How To Live Between Office Visits

So Faith, Hope and Love abide; but the greatest of these is Love.

1 CORINTHIANS 13

For the person and for the species love is the form of behavior having the highest survival value.

ASHLEY MONTAGU

Also by Bernie S. Siegel, M.D.

Love, Medicine & Miracles
Peace, Love & Healing

HOW
TO LIVE
BETWEEN
OFFICE
VISITS

A Guide to Life,
Love and Health

Bernie S. Siegel, M.D.

HarperCollins*Publishers*

Copyright acknowledgments appear on pages 225–228.

HOW TO LIVE BETWEEN OFFICE VISITS: A GUIDE TO LIFE, LOVE AND HEALTH Copyright © 1993 by Bernie S. Siegel. All rights reserved. Printed in the United States of America. No part of this book may be used or reproduced in any manner whatsoever without written permission except in the case of brief quotations embodied in critical articles and reviews. For information address HarperCollins Publishers, Inc., 10 East 53rd Street, New York, NY 10022.

HarperCollins books may be purchased for educational, business or sales promotional use. For information, please write: Special Markets Department, HarperCollins Publishers, Inc., 10 East 53rd Street, New York, NY 10022.

FIRST EDITION

Designed by C. Linda Dingler

Library of Congress Catalog Card Number 92-54736
ISBN 0-06-016800-5

93 94 95 96 97 ◆/RRD 10 9 8 7 6 5 4 3 2 1

To Our Fathers Before Us Who Remain With Us In Spirit
My Father, Simon B. Siegel, who taught me that we are here to make life
easier for each other and that adversity can be a gift.
My Father-in-Law, Adolph L. Stern, who taught me about humor and
courage while imprisoned in a body he could not move.
His advice to the elderly:

> *If you have to fall, remember to fall on something soft.*
> *But I once did—I fell on my wife and broke her leg.*
> *So, that's no good.*
> *Tell them to just fall up.*

I believe that they both fell up.

To those still not finished with me:
My Creator and Co-Creators.

My Mother, Rose, who teaches me about surviving and God's
> *redirections.*
My Wife, Bobbie, the most important contemporary human being in my
> *life and the most attractive lap top computer I know.*
My Mother-in-Law, Merle, and
Our children Jonathan, Jeffrey, Stephen, Carolyn and Keith and their
> *loved ones Judy, Marcia and Roy, for helping me to learn more*
> *about love.*

To the three musketeers who assisted in the birth of this book:
> *Sally Arteseros, who helped in its formation and creation*
> *Victoria Pryor, my agent and more*
> *Carol Cohen, my editor at HarperCollins, and more*
Thank you all for your skill, patience and wisdom.

To Lucille Ranciato, Susan Duffy and all the people who participate in
my life. I wish there were space for all your names to be mentioned.
Please know that you have made a difference in my life. You are all
works of art who inspire me.

A scab
is a beautiful thing—a coin
the body has minted, with an invisible motto:
In God We Trust.
Our body loves us,
and, even while the spirit drifts dreaming,
works at mending the damage that we do. . .

Close your eyes, knowing
that healing is a work of darkness,
that darkness is a gown of healing,
that the vessel of our tremulous venture is lifted
by tides we do not control.
Faith is health's requisite:
we have this fact in lieu
of better proof of le bon Dieu.

— FROM "ODE TO HEALING"
JOHN UPDIKE

Contents

Introduction:
A Guide to Life, Love and Health

One day in the fall of 1977 I was attending a workshop; sitting next to me was a patient of mine with breast cancer. Suddenly she turned to me and said, "You know what I need to know? I need to know how to live between office visits."

I had come to the workshop because of the difficulties I was having as a doctor—not knowing, because of my inadequate training, how to deal with patients as people. Like many physicians, I had built walls around myself as protection from the emotional pain that I was seeing. My training was about how to treat disease. And when you begin to realize you can't cure every disease, you start to feel like a failure.

I know now that we teach what we need to learn. And when this lady spoke to me, I'm sure I was sensing a need in myself to learn how to live too. So I jumped at her question and said, "I'll teach you." I believe that within me a voice was saying, "I need to know this too. We can work on it together." (At the time, I thought we would meet for eight sessions and that in two months we would know how to live. But that short course has extended over fifteen years, and I am still working on the same problem: living.)

I sent letters to a hundred patients, inviting them to participate in a group, to talk about their lives, to draw pictures, to learn about living with their disease. I thought they would tell others, and I expected hundreds of people to respond. But only a dozen women appeared, and so we began with that small group. (And it is no coincidence that it was only women.)

I wanted to find out what was different about these people. What could I, as a surgeon, learn from them? How could other people learn to become "survivors" too? These women were showing me what life was about, showing me that I didn't have the answers, because I hadn't confronted adversity the way they had. I had thought I would be the one teaching and helping them, but I realized that they were the ones who were teaching me.

We began meeting regularly, and eventually longer talks and workshops evolved from our meetings. My wife, Bobbie, gave the group its name: Exceptional Cancer Patients (ECaP). Today ECaP has become a resource and model for support groups all over the world. We are seeing that all disease states are affected by psycho–social interventions. I am thrilled to see recent changes in the attitude of the medical community. Even in hospitals, we are beginning to humanize our approach to people, rather than just taking a mechanistic approach to disease.

After Bobbie and I established ECaP, we began to travel around the country, lecturing and conducting workshops on the art of healing. It had been my hope that my books—*Love, Medicine & Miracles* and *Peace, Love & Healing*—would answer many of the questions that people have. But I did not realize what a book does in terms of making the world aware of its author, and I found that my life was turned upside down. People began to want me, not just my books. At lectures and workshops people came up to talk, and to ask many questions. Others wrote letters or called, out of their need. Sometimes people have spoken to me at inopportune moments. I have not always been able to respond to the questions as fully as I would like.

I have written this book to provide more answers. You have been my teachers and have helped me find answers. Some of the questions included here are about universal problems; others are more specific. Some I may never be able to answer; only you can provide the answers. I want this book to present you with information, but I also want it to be a special support, a comforting voice, an embrace I can't always be there to give. We will learn together.

In the beginning, our workshops were meant for cancer patients, but they have been expanded and are now offered to everyone, for no one is free of afflictions. I realize that I am also speaking to doctors, counselors and students; to families of ill people; to those with AIDS, or lupus or multiple sclerosis. I am speaking to all of us who realize we are mortal and want each day to be precious.

Whether people have won millions of dollars in the lottery or are told they have only twelve months to live, many don't know what to do with their lives. I believe that when your answer to the question of what you would do in the next twelve months is the same whether you have won the lottery or have learned you are going to be dead, then you are really living your life. You are living fully in the moment.

I have some questions for you, too—you will be

presented with some of the questions we ask at workshops. For example: If when you were filling out your income tax form you also had to fill out an application for permission to live, how would you fill out the form? (Stop and think a minute, because if I get to be president, this will definitely be included in your tax form. If we don't accept your reasons, we'll refund your taxes, so that you can have a final good year.) My hope is that your application will make the people reading it want to grant you a longer life.

You will be asked some questions about how you can die with a smile on your face, surrounded by your loved ones. My father did this. I will share his story at the end of the book, but I hope you will think of him in the meantime, and of how you might set up a scene so that you can die surrounded by the people who love you, who will be telling wonderful stories about your life and relationships.

I do want to challenge you, to disturb you and make you think. I'd like this book to be a conversation between us.

Sometimes I think about how much easier life would be for all of us if when we were born we arrived with a book called *A Guide to Life, Love and Health.* (It would be safely sealed in a ziplocked bag for protection during pregnancy, labor and delivery).

Your parents would read the book; it would be handed to you when you were old enough to read; the chapters would cover all the problems you can get into in a lifetime. You would always have a resource.

Of course it would be better not to need a guidebook at all but to have an inner strength and ability with which to face all problems. Then we could simply look into our own hearts, listen to ourselves, draw on our strength and that of our loved ones, and overcome any difficulty in a healthy way. That is what I hope this book will do for you—help you listen to that most important voice of all, the voice within yourself, so that you will learn what true health is.

How do we know how to live our lives? How do we find our path? I notice a theme that keeps recurring over and over again in the stories I hear, and that is of the horse that finds its way home when its reins are released.

In the Grail myth, Parsifal, the knight, rides the horse into the darkest portion of the forest and lets go of the reins. In *Yoga Journal* you read about the chariot being pulled by horses that can, if driven only by the intellect, end up in a ditch—whereas when your intuitive side, the part of you that at a deep level knows the right way, participates, the direction of your life becomes clear.

I think that within each of us is a knowledge of our road, or path. It is intuitive. And yet we so often give it up and don't live our own life but the life that someone else has chosen for us. But we can pay attention to the path that we would like to take. We can stay on the horse but let go of the reins.

The most important direction we can go isn't east or west or north or south, it is inside ourselves. There is a path to your own heart, your own treasure chest, and I would like you to follow it. When people follow it, I hear them say, "I have a disease, but it doesn't have me."

I've always felt that life and nature give us signs when we are on the right path. When we find our way of contributing love to the world, we are in harmony with the world. We are in tune with our intelligence and with nature. So let us find the gift in life.

Often I hear people talk about how cancer can be a wake-up call, a new beginning. Many people have told me that this is what it represents to them. I listen to the parents of a child with cancer say, "This has been a gift and a positive experience in our lives." They are not telling parents of a sick child that the illness is a gift, but they are teaching what may come from it.

A woman named Esther Redelsheimer who had to deal with breast cancer was disturbed by this theme, and she wrote to me:

> I clapped your book shut. I had read enough about the benefits of the illness. My illness was a malignant breast tumor, and I wasn't going to look for any of its benefits. I was sick, not crazy. It wasn't like having a baby. Then the benefits of morning sickness, weight gain and labor were visible. It simply lay in your arms, warm, cute and miraculous, breathing in a sleepy rhythm. Having a baby was exciting, but the tumor was not. The tumor was scary. Surgery, a double mastectomy which wasn't even a certain cure, was just as scary. And after surgery I was weaker than I'd been after labor.

My answer was to share a poem called "Birth," by Leslie Baer, a woman who also had cancer:

Nine months sometimes seems too long
I watch my body change.
Tired, I sit staring out at life
I live within my mind.
Books and music transport me beyond my body.
Stirring within me a new life.
Nine months finally pass.
I give birth to my child.
All the discomfort and pain is now justified.
Radiation and chemotherapy.
Twelve months sometimes seems too long.
I watch my body change.
I sit staring out at life.
I live within my mind.
Books and music transport me beyond my body.
Stirring within me new life.

Twelve months finally pass.
I give birth to myself.
All the discomfort and pain is now justified.

Life is a labor pain, worthwhile if we can give birth to ourselves. But I see people who in a sense have died to stay alive. I'm talking about your becoming who you didn't want to be, because of pressure from parents or other authority figures—you become the doctor, the teacher, the plumber, the housewife, even if the work and role are meaningless to you. And then one day you are told you have a year to live. For some of you, learning that you are mortal finally gives you permission to live your life. And so the teacher quits his job and moves to the seashore, the doctor picks up a flute, the housewife goes back to college, the plumber becomes a sculptor. They let the untrue self die and give birth to their true selves. You can commit suicide without hurting your body.

You don't have to have permission to do this. We are all mortal. Don't wait until someone tells you that you have cancer or AIDS. Start living. Give yourself a new date of birth.

Then the psychological and spiritual healing process can happen, and it may be accompanied by a physical cure as well. The physical change is the by-product of your giving birth to yourself, free of the diseases of the past. Don't be angry at yourself or blame yourself for the ways in which you have survived and met your needs. All symptoms are honorable. They redirect you. Move forward. The past is over.

It is interesting that Esther Redelsheimer, who started out angry and asked about the benefits of being sick, concluded her letter by saying that her life had taken a new direction:

Regardless of what I do—volunteer work, gardening, or if it's something special like going to a symphony—each day offers me a lot of meaning and opportunities. I've decided to find the meaning and take advantage of the opportunities. My outlook has been contagious and my husband seems to have caught it. I wish I didn't have to admit it because I should have been able to celebrate life without getting cancer. But my new appreciation as well as my husband's is a benefit of the illness.

As long as I'm confessing to benefits, I've got to add that I no longer iron shirts. While I was in the hospital, we found it easier and even better to take them to the cleaners. And since my reconstructive surgery, I can go braless if I choose—sometimes, I do. I am well now. Still, if I get sick again, I'd rather not talk benefits.

I know that environment and heredity play a role in your ability to live a full life and be healthy. I realize that you may have been born with an affliction or exposed to a toxic environment. But we are talking about the choices you make that heal your life. So quadriplegics imprisoned in their bodies can lead healed lives just as well as epileptics and cerebral palsied people, and so can individuals who are incarcerated in prison, and those with cancer and AIDS and every other affliction. They can lead healed lives, and become healers to those around them.

I see a quadriplegic artist hold a paintbrush in his mouth and create beauty and love. I know an individual with athetoid cerebral palsy who cannot control any part of her body. The only way she can send me a letter is to be tied in a chair and gagged so that she doesn't drool on, or fall and bang into, the word processor. Then she types with her nose on the word processor. She sends me a Christmas card that reads, "Let's spend Christmas with Jesus helping people less fortunate than we."

The inspiration isn't because the afflictions of these people make ours seem less severe; it is because they

are teaching us. The issue isn't who has the worst problem—we all have problems, and we can inspire each
other by confronting them.

I'm told that in one of the episodes of "The
Untouchables" Eliot Ness captures a paraplegic gangster who is sitting in a wheelchair. Ness asks him why
he became a criminal, and the gangster says, "I'm
handicapped, what kind of living could I earn? I had to
become a gangster. What could I do?" Ness pulls from
his pocket a newspaper announcing Franklin Delano
Roosevelt's election as president. There is a picture of
Roosevelt in a wheelchair. And he shows this to the
criminal and says, "Well, for one thing, you could have
run for the presidency."

We are so afraid of taking a risk, of being nothing,
that some of us actually kill ourselves rather than live
our lives. A conference I recently attended was called
"The Unlimited Human." I think we are just beginning
to reach out and understand that for human beings the
question is not one of limits, but of possibilities.

Yes, you have to be willing to take a risk. A man
told me that he was thinking of writing a book called
Second Lives, about what people have done because of
cancer, heart disease, or violence that has struck them.
But I don't want people to need a second life; I want
you to live this one now.

Life is an opportunity for you to contribute love in
your own way. I'd like you to find the strength that I
know is there inside you to draw on. Then use that
strength and energy and live fully. You will realize that
you are a sphere whose center is everywhere and
whose circumference is nowhere. Just as one thought
affects your entire body, so do you affect everyone else
when you change. So give birth to yourself and begin
your life. Let the river of your life flow freely and
deeply, and let the pebbles of your love fall into the
water to create ripples that will touch us all.

1
Help, Where Do I Go From Here?

This is the true joy in life, the being used for a purpose recognized by yourself as a mighty one; the being thoroughly worn out before you are thrown on the scrap heap. . .

—GEORGE BERNARD SHAW
EPISTLE DEDICATORY TO MAN AND SUPERMAN

I don't want to be saved, I want to be spent.

—FRITZ PERLS
FOUNDER OF GESTALT THERAPY

We Are Perfectly Imperfect

I receive many letters, and often they end with these words: "Help, where do I go from here?" This question sometimes comes from people who are ill, or it may be asked by those who are well again and are wondering what to do with their lives.

One lady wrote saying,

> I was told many times that I had not long to live, and as I was very ill I thought they might be right. So I made out a will, gave away my valued treasures to family and friends, I bought a dog, took more vitamins, started exercising and eating better, laughed more, and put in a backyard wildlife habitat, my life's desire. If I was going to die, I might as well die doing all the things I wanted to do.
>
> I lived, and now I'm going to kill myself by never slowing down. Help, where do I go from here?

People like this are easy to help. I can write them a prescription: "Take a nap." They are living their lives fully: burning up, not burning out. They are spending their lives.

When you are burning up you are living your life, and taking a nap or a vacation will provide you with energy and strength to go on. But burning out, a simple rest won't cure. Burning out means misusing yourself, dying with much left over in the candleholder. It means never really having lived fully.

Many people are in incredible pain. They are over-whelmed by life's difficulties and seeming unfairness. They have lost their power. So when a book comes out on how to commit suicide, it becomes a bestseller. But if you regain your power, you regain your life and your death and you don't have to be afraid. How do you gain that power? That is a question that I hope we can explore together.

I know that part of the answer lies in realizing that we don't have to be perfect.

In Martin Buber's "Tales of the Hasidim," there is a story about how each of us should carry in one pocket a card with these words: "For my sake was the world created." And in another pocket, a card saying, "I am earth and ashes." Both statements are true. Together they say that we are perfectly imperfect. You can reach into whichever pocket is appropriate for the day.

I like to keep that thought in mind, because it is the process of living that is important and that we are all struggling with—not the product, or the result. In fact, we can say that the process **is** the product—that's what living your life means. Raising your child, tending your garden, driving the bus, running the elevator, loving the world in your way—these are the things that are significant, not the gold watch you receive when you retire, or the diploma. It is the experience of living that is important, not searching for a meaning. We bring meaning by how we love the world.

We will never be finished products. And once we realize that we don't have to be perfect, we can reveal our vulnerability and ask for help. We can change our idea of what being "independent" is.

The Real Meaning of Independence

Many of us are brought up to think we have to solve our problems by ourselves, to put on "a brave front" and be strong. But if you think that trying to do it all makes you independent, you're wrong. What this does is exhaust you and make you vulnerable to illness, and it leads you to resent the world. You end up with few true relationships and little support.

Being independent doesn't mean that you don't need other people in your life. We all do, to make our lives significant. Independence means knowing your ability to deal with adversity as well as expressing feelings, asking for help when appropriate, learning to share your needs. It means not being lonely even when you are alone. It means developing into a full and complete human being, in the healthiest sense of the word.

What is it within us that says, "I'm weak and vulnerable if I ask for help, even for directions when I'm lost"? My wife, Bobbie, has a one-liner that always brings a roar of laughter at our workshops, especially from the women. She asks, "Why did the tribes in Israel wander in the desert for forty years?" The answer is: "Because even then, men couldn't ask directions." But we can begin to understand that we can ask for help.

Dr. Walter Menninger, a friend and medical school classmate of mine, wrote an article called "The Mental

Health Imperative: Learning from Adversity." In it he says, "Acknowledge that everyone has limits. . . and learn to read your own signals that the limits are being approached or gone beyond. And be comfortable in asking for help when your limits are surpassed."

If your family didn't teach you this, it can be hard to set new behavior patterns, and reach out.

Reverend William Chidester, a minister we know, spent his whole life giving. I have seen this happen many times, with people in many professions. But when he became ill, he learned how much love could come back to him. He and his wife had been babysitters of ours in our home in Connecticut in the early 1970s. They subsequently moved to Ohio, where he developed a liver disease for which there was no specific cure or treatment, except a transplant when his liver function deteriorated. For many years he remained basically asymptomatic, working on the illness with self-healing techniques learned from books; these included meditating and visualizing. He wrote me to say that from the beginning, he and his wife, Sharon,

> . . . decided that we would be as active and positive in every aspect of the illness that we could. We asked a lot of questions. I did as much exercise as I could. We felt that a transplant was the right thing to do and that it was going to work. In the hospital, I made one decision which helped remove much guilt. I decided I was doing all I could do and that if there were any rejection, that was something I couldn't control. I was in charge of the spiritual, psychological and physical aspects of my recovery, but I couldn't force my body not to reject the liver.
> During my hospital stay I cannot begin to tell you what kind of support I received from friends. What has been impressed upon me in ways that I

will never forget is this—as a minister I spend much of my time caring for and about others. I am affirmed in the process of doing this. So here I am working hard to earn people's love, trust and admiration by being the best possible minister I can. Yet I was never able to do enough. Then I find something I can't do, function with my own liver, and it is out of my weakness that the grace of God is revealed. Because of what I can't do, I have been affirmed in these people's support and love beyond anything I thought possible.

Ministers, physicians, nurses, all health-care providers—and, for that matter, every one of us—can learn from this. Our patients, our loved ones, our friends can be a resource.

When you reveal your vulnerability you help yourself as well as others. What you find is that everybody around you needs help and that they begin to share with you things they have never told you before.

How can you reveal your vulnerability? Broken hearts don't show—when you walk down the street or attend a workshop you can look around and have no idea who has a broken heart. But you know who has a broken leg, a broken arm, a limp. Those things are visible. And so tomorrow, when you go out, wear a neck brace, limp, and use a cane, and watch what people do for you and how they relate to you.

I saw this at the hospital when I shaved my head. From my previous books, many of you know what lead me to shave my head. I learned that it was symbolic of uncovering feelings and spiritual rebirth, like a baby's head or a monk's. I was now different. People started talking to me and telling me things that they had never told me before, and I had known them for years. I was now wounded and safe to talk to.

When you share what is in your heart, others will share with you and help you. You will actually become more independent because you will be able to accept help and know it is there when you need it. Knowing you can care for yourself gives you independence. It's part of being independent to say, "I have resources, I have people who can respond. I don't have to use the same person or my family over and over again." You will build up a network of people who will help you remain independent. And you will do that for them also.

For some people relationships are frightening. I asked one woman how she described her cancer, and she said, "It's a failure." I said, "What do you mean?" She said, "Well, my body has failed me." I said, "No, what I'm interested in is how the word **failure** fits your life." She said, "My parents committed suicide when I was a child. I must have been a failure as a child."

It is hard to form relationships if you have had that kind of childhood, because you're afraid that others will hurt you. This woman is not someone who asks for help or who would let you hug her. But because of her cancer she has changed, and the walls came down. She realized that other people have troubles too. I can help them, she thought, and she really was able to, because of her own difficulties. And then she could accept the help of others.

Please, don't get cancer to learn some of these lessons.

Finding Your True Path: Getting on the Universe's Schedule

One man told me that he feels he has to "get everything finished and in order" before he can have peace of mind or relax. I know what this is like, because years ago I used to make lists. As a physician I was always on call and would have lists of things I could do in fifteen minutes in case I got paged and had to run to the hospital, or things that could be done on a day off when one of my partners was covering for me. As the nature of my work began to change and I became more open to my feelings, I tore up the lists. The truth is, if a pipe bursts at home, that's suddenly on your list—you have to do something about it. If the roof leaks, you can put a bucket under the leak and get to it later. But get back to living, and don't let a list run your life. You will never get everything finished. Life is about learning how to live without things being in order, and who knows what order is anyway?

On our family car we have a bumper sticker that reads, "Everything in the universe is subject to change and everything is on schedule." If you're on the universe's schedule, everything is in order. You are now in God's country, like nature. Nature is chaotic, yet orderly. And your body is made to survive the chaos, the internal changes in weather. It isn't perfectly regular and orderly every minute.

When you look at the new theories of physics and chaos, you begin to see a pattern within the body. In *Chaos: Making a New Science*, James Gleick writes about how a living organism creates a stream of order out of all the chaos and disorder around it. We are built for chaotic, unpredictable changes and behavior. Change is really what we thrive on. We would get in trouble if everything were exact all the time—the weather, or our heartbeat or blood pressure. That sort of precision would be more threatening, because then if things varied, we wouldn't be able to handle the change.

Biological systems can participate in change, and peace of mind can come without everything being on schedule. There are practical things you can do to help yourself accept change, such as keeping a journal of your feelings or expressing how you feel when you don't have everything under control. It could mean joining a group and talking to other people who have the same feelings and learning to meditate and do imagery and deep breathing so that you have resources in those moments when things are difficult. These things will get you back on the universe's schedule and help you to stop judging everything as right or wrong.

It could be that a delay will save your life—if you miss a plane that crashes, or if while you are waiting for an X-ray for which the technician is late you meet someone who gives you great advice about your illness. If you had been "on schedule" you would have missed that person. Remember that all the clocks in Heaven have their hands removed; they say, "One, two, three, four, who cares?"

Bobbie and I travel a lot, and if we get home and the furnace or the air conditioning isn't working, we try to get repair people into the house within a day to get things fixed before we fly off again. That can get complicated, and I do get emotional about it. But I understand that this is my life. I am not a victim. It is my choice to live in this way. And you and I know that all those things we were tormented about two months ago don't seem so important anymore, and that more things are going to happen. (When people enter Heaven and look back at earth, the most frequently asked question is, "Why was I so serious back there?")

Cheryl Parsons Darnell, a wonderful woman from Texas, wrote some beautiful poems; her husband sent me several of them after her death. One was entitled "The Lessons of Texas," and it says a lot about learning to live with life's difficulties.

In the poem, she speaks about how she grew up in Texas—rains, floods, droughts, hurricanes and twisters—and the way to live with them. She concludes the poem with these lines:

I grew up in Texas, where you learn
    To keep candles and flashlight batteries,
Where you learn about weather,
    Love and life and how to ride it out.

So get your candles and flashlight batteries together—all of your resources, the things that you need—and learn to ride life out. You don't have to hang on to the reins to ride it out.

Remember what you have survived. Think of what you are capable of doing. Being in touch with your feelings and needs, participating in life in your way, choosing happiness and carrying hope and peace within you—these are the things that make life meaningful. If peace is in your mind, it will come to your entire life. You can choose to keep your power, you can choose happiness, and you can say yes and no at the appropriate times.

Learning to Say No to the World and Yes to Yourself

My first response when someone asks how he or she can learn to say no is to suggest that the question be changed to: "How can I say yes to myself and value myself?" Look at yourself in the mirror and start saying yes. Then, saying no to the things you don't want to do will become easier. I am not asking you to be selfish; I am asking you to do what you want to do to love the world, so that you are contributing to the world.

People are sometimes surprised when I display anger. But I think that saying no, displaying anger (and I'm not talking about resentment and hatred, I'm talking about simple anger), is healthy. If somebody steps on your foot, do you say, "Excuse me, my foot is under yours"? Or do you say, "Hey, you're on my foot. Get off. You're hurting me"?

Anger is a defense of your uniqueness and individuality. In the Bible it's called righteous indignation. So if you don't like the idea of getting angry, it's okay to get righteously indignant.

In a sense, saying no means defending yourself. Are you willing to be used and abused? Well, if you're not worth anything, if you have no self-esteem, no self-love, then you will have trouble saying no. But the moment you think that you and your time are important, you may display some anger toward people for trying to use you. And then they'll be surprised. "Oh, you're supposed to be a lover." Being a loving person doesn't mean that you're a doormat. And so after being angry or saying no to somebody, I can still give them a hug.

When I say no, it doesn't mean that I don't care about you. It's just that I have something that is more significant for me right now. This is my life, my time, and I want to use it in my way. People may begin to understand that the "no" comes from a different place; it has nothing to do with not valuing them, it has to do with my caring about and valuing myself.

When people would like to manipulate you, you have to assert yourself. You may feel it easier and safer to be sick, because then others will feel sorry for you, and you can control them and say no without guilt. I can also guarantee it is easier to be dead. Then nobody will bother you. But what an opportunity you'll have given up! Rather than use an illness or gain permission from it, there are healthier ways to achieve your goals.

Saying no conveys the message "I'm living my life." Don't wait until you have ten minutes to live to say it for the first time.

If you have had to put others' needs before your own to survive, it will be hard to learn to say no. Two-year-old children say it all the time. But if you were given the message that it was destructive and threatening or poor behavior and bad manners to say no, it will be hard for you as an adult. People might not like you. But you have to erase those old, hypnotic, parental, authoritarian messages that we die by.

Practice saying no, and observe that the world will not fall apart. It may even be healthier.

When you learn to say no, illness doesn't need to say it for you. You can change your way of responding to the world. When the telephone rings or your beeper sounds, you can let the ring or beeper become a "bell of mindfulness," as Thich Nhat Hanh, the Buddhist monk, writes of in his wonderful book *Peace Is Every Step*. He suggests that when you hear such a sound—a temple bell, or three rings on the telephone; it can be any sound, or vision—breathe in peace. Think "This sound brings me back to myself." Then the ring of the phone can bring you peace and love, and when you answer it, you will be in a different place. The call becomes a gift. One woman, about to commit suicide, got up to answer the phone. The call saved her because she realized she didn't have to commit suicide, she just had to stop answering the telephone.

My mother shared an experience with me. One day many years ago, when I was a child, she and my father took her mother to the doctor. The doctor looked at my mother and said, "You look sicker than your mother. Come in here." He examined her and found that she had rheumatic fever, and he immediately put her in an ambulance and sent her to the hospital. My mother said that as she was wheeled into the hospital, she looked around and said, "Oh, what a relief." Yes, she was killing herself taking care of others. She had four siblings and she could have asked for help.

I meet many people who say, "How can I take a vacation? What would the neighbors say?" If my mother had gone to Florida for a week or had just insisted that one of her sisters or brothers take over, what would have happened? Would people have said,

"What a terrible child she is, not helping her mother"? Or would she have felt guilty? But we need to be able to say no if we are going to survive, and not have to get so sick that we can be hospitalized instead of taking a vacation or speaking up for ourselves.

If you want to make your friends and family healthier, teach them to say no. How? That's easy. Make a list of all the things you want done in your life—mowing the lawn, shopping, painting the house. Call your neighbors and relatives and ask them to do the work. Ninety percent of them will say yes. Then they'll start calling you, because they'll want you to repay them for the time they spent. When they call, ask, "Did you do what you did for me out of love?" If they say "Yes," say, "Then you were rewarded." And if they say "I didn't do it out of love, I felt obligated," you say, "Then next time say no. I'm teaching you how to stay healthy."

Confronting Your Fears

Living and staying healthy requires confronting your fears. As you learn how to fight for your life and deal with fears, peace of mind occurs, because you know you can handle what will come. But it is not uncommon as you work on this to ask, "How can I get over the fear of recurrence, of always living on the edge, waiting for the other shoe to drop?" I was asked this specific question at a workshop recently, and it made me think of a poem that one woman wrote, saying that when all her hair grew back she would do the things she had put off.

I told her, "Don't wait until your hair grows back. Do it now. Because one never knows what the future will bring. Don't postpone living. Don't say, 'Some day my day will come.' Live now." Life exists only in the moment.

What are your fears? Truly define them. Do not be vague about it. Don't say things like, "I'm afraid of dying." I don't know what that means. Sit down and say, "What am I really afraid of? Is it the pain, the treatment, the not being in control, the worry about what the treatment will do to me? Am I afraid no one will take care of me? Or is it that I'm really afraid of living and making choices?" There is an enormous difference between fear and grief or sadness. Grief or sadness is normal when one is having a difficult time.

It is important to look at the metaphors for your fears, to embrace them and learn from them. In our workshops I work with imagery, and one image I ask people to visualize is that of an infant crying. Imagine that there is a nursery in your home and there is a baby in a crib crying. Picture that baby as your greatest fear or problem. Pick it up, caress it, and see what happens to your fear. Be aware that it isn't you—hold it up away from you. You are not the fear; you are separate from it. In this way you can begin to go into your own darkness and embrace your fear and pain and learn from them. Do you have the faith in yourself to do this? That is the key.

As Susan Bach, a Jungian therapist and author, says, "When you compress charcoal, it becomes a diamond." When you are under pressure, if you are willing to allow the darkness, pain, and difficulties to teach you, then you too can produce great gifts.

In *The Joseph Campbell Companion: Reflections on the Art of Living*, Joseph Campbell is quoted as saying:

It is only by going down into the abyss
that we recover the treasures of life.
Where you stumble,
there lies your treasure.
The very cave you are afraid to enter
turns out to be the source of
what you were looking for.

Such wisdom has been imparted over many years, in many forms. Campbell also shared:

> A bit of advice
> given to a young Native American
> at the time of his initiation:
> "As you go the way of life,
> you will see a great chasm.
> Jump.
> It is not as wide as you think."

I remember a story about a young woman who was helping her father; he was a builder and she was assisting him in the woods, cutting trees. One day she saw a bottle, and it looked as though something were jumping up and down in it. So she picked up the bottle, thinking that a little lizard or frog had been trapped. Then she heard a voice from inside the bottle saying, "Let me out."

She opened the bottle, and out came a genie, who began threatening her. It said, "I have to kill you, that's the rule. Whoever lets me out, I have to kill." And the young lady, who was very frightened, said bravely, "That's nonsense, you never came out of a bottle. Look at you, and look at the size of the bottle. I have to get back to work with my father." The genie said, "Wait a minute. I can demonstrate that what I am saying is true." She said, "Show me." So the genie went back into the bottle, and she quickly put the cork in. She started to walk away when she heard the genie yelling, "Wait, wait. If you let me out again I'll do you a favor."

Now the test. You have rebottled your symptoms and fears by confronting the genie, but are you willing to go further for true healing? Do you trust your ability? Do you have faith in yourself? The young woman did, so she pulled the cork again, because she knew she could handle whatever came her way. And the genie said, "I was telling the truth. Here is a cloth. Rub it on a wound, it will heal. Rub it on metal, it will turn to silver." She rubbed the cloth on her axe, which became silver; she rubbed it on the wound of a tree trunk, and it healed. She went home and used the silver to pay her tuition to medical school and today is one of the world's greatest physicians and healers.

When we confront our genie, when we confront what threatens us, we become healers and teachers to all those around us. Do not be afraid.

What would you do if you did have a recurrence, if your cancer came back? Think about it. If the will to live is still in you, you will find a new therapy, a new hope. If it isn't there, you may decide not to have treatment. One woman who decided to stop her therapy was in conflict over the choice and how to tell her doctor. She said, "I had a dream the night before I was to see my doctor, and in the dream a white cat appeared. I said to the cat, 'What is your name?' And the cat said, 'My name is Miracle.'" The woman told me, "I knew it was the right choice to stop treatment. Today, eight years later, I could resume treatment. It wasn't a question of its being right or wrong for a lifetime, but for me at that moment."

This is one of the qualities of exceptional patients —they are not afraid to make choices related to their lives. This woman made a choice about what was right for her in the present. Her decision was not based on what would happen in the future, whether she was right or wrong, or whether the disease would come back.

If you have a recurrence you will grieve. Grief is appropriate. You may have other feelings, too, like anger. You can use the anger; it is energy. When people are angry—at their disease, or at what I've written— I'm happy. When they feel guilt or despair, shame or blame, then it's hard for them to change, because there is no energy for change. Passion leads to change.

One man came home and said to his wife when he learned he had cancer of the pancreas, "Cancel my dental appointment." And she said, "You're not going to sit in the living room and die for the next six months." He lived almost another two years because of his wife. He made his whole community proud of him because he got back to living, took on challenges and far exceeded anyone's expectations.

I received in the mail a poem called "The Good Thing About Cancer," written by a lady named Patsy Barrineau. She is dead now, but she left this wise and beautiful message:

> The good thing about cancer
> is that it speaks
> in short sentences.
> I listen attentively
> as malignancy whispers:
>
>
> Applaud yourself.
> Hold his hand longer.
> Hug her.
> Buy it.
> Say it.
> Touch.
> Kiss.
> Smile.
> Scream.
> Laugh.
> Cry.
> Enjoy.
> Live.
> Yes.

Living Your Life Fully

How can you live your life the way you want without feeling selfish? Many of us are brought up to please others, and in doing that we stifle parts of ourselves.

But living your life is not selfish. Ask yourself how you can contribute love to the world. That's really what the question should be.

You are mortal, and you have a limited amount of time on earth. You may not be thinking about how you use each day. My definition of how you use your day isn't "What can I get today?" but rather "What can I give today?" When you become clear about how you want to love the world, then you will be living your life without being selfish.

Niro Asistent, who learned she had AIDS and was told she had eighteen months to live, said, "I wrote the number of days left in my life on my refrigerator and said I'd make every day precious." She didn't say she would be selfish every day, she said she'd make every day precious. (About seven years after she was supposed to be dead she wrote a book, called *How I Survive AIDS*, about her experience. She is HIV negative today.)

If you act from love, rather than out of duty, you will be amazed at the results. If you want to do something out of love, do it. You will be rewarded. If you volunteer two hours a week out of love to do things for people you're unrelated to, you'll live a longer, healthier life. If you are holding a lighted candle and I come to you with my unlit candle and light it from yours, you will have no less light. Giving from love is like that. But if you're doing what you don't want to do, out of guilt, you'll end up shortening your life. It would be a pleasure to be sick or die and free yourself from the burden. But the universe's energy isn't depleted, just as that candlelight isn't.

If your parents said they wanted you to be a teacher or a doctor, and you wanted to be an actor or a writer, is it selfish for you to have a choice of your own? No. It's your life. Live it. Become what you would like to be. Because if you don't, watch what will happen to you, and how you feel about yourself and your family. I am asking you to live your life, not just to exist.

Tullia Forlani Kidde wrote to me, describing how she came from Europe to Canada and finally to the United States. She married, pursued a career and then was diagnosed as having cancer, with six to twelve months to live. She said,

I remember how I stood in bewilderment, unable to grasp the reality of what was happening. I kept repeating to myself, "this was supposed to be a beginning." Gradually my answer came: I had to look to myself for help. My body was sick and my emotions were out of control, but I realized that my soul, the very essence of my being, was whole, intact. I could learn to listen to my inner voice—to the wisdom within, which was always there, and which I had dismissed, doubted and overruled. I became my own project, my own immediate goal. I had lived my life outwardly, but now there was a world to discover within myself; a world which didn't require people, books and external aid. I learned to listen to the silence. Slowly my focus changed, my anguish lessened, my acceptance of my condition grew. I didn't need to learn how to die with dignity but to live for today. I taught myself to appreciate the smallest things that were available to me, taking nothing for granted. I learned to forgive myself and others and to say thank you from the heart. I was alive. For today. I started looking at the world in ways I never had before, and perceiving things I never knew existed. My motto became "I shall overcome." I knew in my heart that my healing had begun.

It was a beginning and a rebirth for her. She wrote this letter fourteen years after she was told she had a year to live.

It is my hope that as she has done, you will begin to live your life, listen to your inner voice, and find your true self, the true "I am." I am talking about finding what you love for yourself and in yourself.

Think back to a time in your childhood when you were doing what you loved to do, and how each day flew by. Hours seemed like minutes. When you love your work, when you love your life, then every day is like that. You can recapture that sense of living fully in the moment. The Kingdom of Heaven is open to the child. You can find your Heaven on earth if you return to your childlike nature.

We can learn so much from stories and myths. The child in "The Emperor's New Clothes" reported that the emperor had no clothes on, and his father supported him. The father could have smacked him on the head and said, "You embarrass me. I'll never take you to a parade again." But he said, "Listen to the innocent one." And the people whispered, "The Emperor doesn't have anything on."

I have seen this kind of behavior in my office. I love when the children come in and say, "You don't have any hair on your head," and the parents say, "Shhh! Don't say anything." This is something that is so obvious; it is right in front of people, and yet the adults are trying to ignore it. They are uncomfortable. Their ability to love and communicate is blocked, but not the child's.

Joseph Campbell in an interview in *An Open Life* tells us that Friedrich Nietzsche said:

There are three stages to the spirit. The first is that of the camel. The camel gets down on its knees and says "Put a load on me." This is the condition of youth and learning. When the camel is well loaded, he gets to his feet and runs out into the desert. This is the place where he is going to be alone to find himself, and he is transformed into a lion. And the function and deed of the lion is to kill the dragon. And that dragon's name is Thou Shalt. On every scale of the dragon is written a law, some dating from 2000 B.C., others from yesterday's newspapers. When the camel is well loaded, the lion is potent and the dragon is killed. You see, there are two quite different things. One is submission, obedience, learning; the other is strength and assertion, and when the dragon is killed, the lion is transformed into a child. In Nietzsche's words, "A wheel rolling out of its own center." That's what the child represents in this mystical language. The human being has recovered that spontaneity and innocence and thoughtlessness of rules which are so marvelous in childhood. The little one who comes up and says absolutely embarrassing things to the stranger who is visiting your house, that's the child. Not the obedient child, but the innocent one who is spontaneous and has the courage to live its impulses.

Let that childlike spirit within you guide you. In allowing yourself to be who you really are, you can heal the spirit and the body.

We have to be able to complete all of the stages of development that Joseph Campbell talks about. And we need to learn to live not for the future, nor to lament the past, but to live in the present.

Resetting Your Clock: Learning to Live in the Moment

To reset your clock it helps if you're a little strange and hear voices inside your head. This happens to me frequently, but the voices help me to not be a victim.

(When I told this to a lady she gave me a pin that said, "I hope the noise in my head isn't disturbing you.") When I am at a professional meeting, or a workshop, I think about what I want to share. If I'm worried about what people will think and are afraid to talk freely and openly, a voice will say as I am getting up to speak, "You could die on the way home." I know that if this happened I would feel terrible that I did not share what was in my heart. So I speak, knowing that if I don't survive the day, I have said what I needed to say. What others feel or what critics might say is their problem, not mine. Your awareness of your own mortality can save you from being timid. (But if you do this for applause from the audience and critics, you will only make yourself more vulnerable.)

A young woman worked with me when she was a medical student. Her family wrote to tell me that just as she was to start practice, she was stung by a wasp. A friend found her at home in shock and took her to the intensive-care unit at the local hospital, but she died there three days later of anaphylactic shock. She is in my mind when I think about how uncertain life is, and how we should all strive to live in the present—it really is all we have.

Once you literally accept that you could die on the way home, you begin to free yourself to act in a way that says, "This is me. This is how I feel like contributing." Again, this is not selfish. When you accept your mortality, more humor and love come into your life. Your sense of your own mortality promotes healthy, humorous behavior and uniqueness and individuality—it doesn't hide these things.

I ask people to learn to live in small time segments, because I see over and over again that happy people are living in the moment—that they are, in a sense, getting as close to Heaven on earth as possible. When we can begin to live without always being aware of the clock and just enjoy the here and now, we change ourselves and our bodies. One woman told me that the day she suddenly had a sense of living in the moment, she was sitting in a chair by an open window, with a breeze coming in. For the first time in her life she was aware of feeling air on her skin. Before this, she had screened out such impressions, living for the future, concentrating on what was coming next. Another woman, who was about to commit suicide, suddenly noticed the snow and the blue sky, and their beauty saved her life.

Living in the moment doesn't mean you may not schedule things and have plans for the future. But when your plans are redirected, maybe God is trying to get you on the universe's schedule, trying to get you in touch with your intuitive side.

A man told me that when he retired, "All of a sudden people started talking to me in drugstores. Dogs were friendlier." Without realizing it, of course, he was the one who had changed and was now open.

I can remember being mystified in a philosophy and religion course in college by St. Augustine's statement that one must love in order to see—my thought being that love was blind. Later I realized that lovers are open to the world. If you can remain open, you will accept things when you see them. Even if you don't understand why something has happened, you will know it has and can make note of it and observe rather than reject. Carl Jung said, "We cannot change anything unless we accept it."

If you are open to new truths, spontaneous and unexpected things can happen; mysteries get solved. So many discoveries have been made accidentally, while scientists were in pursuit of something else. Off to the side would be a little truth they might have rushed past without noticing, had they not been open. Our son Jeffrey said one day that someone was "too closed-minded" to be scientific. I thought that was a wonderful comment; it conveys the fact that if we close ourselves up, whether about religion or disease or science, we'll never learn. I'm talking about being open to mystery, not to magic or to miracles. Magic and miracles do not lend themselves to solutions. Mysteries do, and some day they will all be solved.

I have received letters from people who are in prison and are choosing to live a healed life. One man wrote, "I felt condemned to die and was sitting around waiting to go. Now I work eight hours a day of hard labor (moving concrete slabs manually) and look forward to tomorrow. Instead of waiting to die, I now wait to live."

You can be incarcerated in an institution or imprisoned in your body. But the choice to live comes from you, not from your surroundings. If you are waiting to live until you get out of prison, or until your hair grows back, you are postponing life.

My greatest teachers are the afflicted. Go to them in jails, in hospitals, and ask, "Why do you want to live?" I walked through hospital corridors, going into rooms, asking people who had things I was afraid of, "Why do you want to live? How do you manage?" They were always honest and willing to help. Some said, "Sit down, I'll tell you." Others said, "Come back, I'll make a list for you." What impressed me was that the list did not contain pages of philosophical discussion about the meaning of life. They said things that were so simple. "I painted a picture," said someone with no fingers; a brush had to be tied to her hand. "I looked out the window, and it is a beautiful day." "The nurse rubbed my back." "My family called and are coming to see me." The lists just went on with simple daily events. And I began to realize that this is really what life is about.

A young man who spoke eloquently about living in the moment was Mark Rakowski. He was a football player at my alma mater, Colgate, but he developed leukemia soon after graduation. Mark's former football coach and the Director of Athletics, Fred Dunlap, and his wife wrote about Mark; their story appeared in the Colgate paper. They described how the members of the football team had always been impressed with Mark, with his spirit and will to live, and how the team wanted to give him an award. He couldn't receive the award in the stadium; it would have been unwise to expose him to all the people with his low white count due to chemotherapy. So the award was given to him in the locker room before the game. He told the players:

> When I was playing football I always thought I gave everything I had on every play, especially during my senior year. But now that I'm not playing anymore, I know that I didn't; I just thought I did. Now that I have finished my playing, I'd give anything to play again and really go all out. Some day you will feel the same way. So, don't leave anything in here today. Leave it all out there on the field.

Needless to say, everyone gave his all, and they upset Army 22–20.

Mark later died of complications following a bone marrow transplant. But there are many people who will never forget him and his example.

And that's what I share with you, my friend. Play your game to the fullest.

Live as if you were dying; write as if you were dying. In an article in the *New York Times Book Review* (May 28, 1989) called "Write Till You Drop," Annie Dillard said:

> Write as if you were dying. At the same time, assume you write for an audience consisting solely of terminal patients. That is, after all, the case. What would you begin writing if you knew you

would die soon? What could you say to a dying person that would not enrage by its triviality?

I like to use this exercise at workshops, and now I ask you: What would you write about if you knew you had only six months to live? What would you want to share with others, to get in touch with feelings that lie deep inside you? When we do this we all begin to focus on what we love best.

Stop; close your eyes. In the darkness you may lose your sight and develop insight. Helen Keller often asked this question of people: "If you had three days to see, what would you choose to see in those days?" I think that your choice will teach you about what you truly love in your life.

Identifying Your True Feelings

Most people have difficulty identifying their true joys, needs and desires because they have stopped paying attention to their feelings. When you say to a child, "What do you want to do today?" or, "What do you want to be when you grow up?" you get answers. When our five children were younger and we were all on vacation, I would ask each morning, "What do you want to do today?" I got thirty or forty answers. By nightfall we had done only twenty-eight things, I was exhausted, and they were mad. I had to learn to stop asking. So each day I would come up with an activity that we could all enjoy, and they'd invariably join in. They were open and alive to possibilities. Ask an adult, "What do you want to do today?" and you're likely to hear, "Well, I don't know, what would you like to do?" And if you suggest something, you'll hear, "Well, all right, if that's what you want."

When you are not in touch with your feelings it can be hard to distinguish between a healthy attraction and an unhealthy addiction. But if you can get in touch with your childlike qualities, your body will let you know if you are making the right choices and if your feelings are genuine. A healthy attraction makes you feel good, even though it may tire you. An unhealthy addiction is in control of you. You're driven, whether you want to be or not. This can involve a substance; it can mean your work; it can mean doing things for others—things that take control of your life away from you. None of these can replace love. If you talk to volunteers, to people who are willing to serve, and you talk to addicts, and you ask, "How do you feel after taking a drug, how do you feel after you volunteer out of love to help someone?" the answers will sound alike. Both groups will be on a high. But it's a lot healthier to get high on helping than on drugs. When you get high on helping, you will see physical as well as psychological improvement. (As Bobbie says, "Volunteer for the health of it.")

An unhealthy addiction may have started out being something healthy. I know people who have started to jog because it's good for them and it feels good to exercise. But the next thing you know they're preparing for marathons, compulsively training for hours a day, disrupting their lives. This is unhealthy.

Addictions—and this can include taking drugs, making money, exercising for hours a day and a whole host of other things—can be seen as means of trying to gain love and feelings that should come in healthier ways. They are really replacements for the love we wish we had. We couldn't control the source of love when we were children, and we try to do it now.

In her book *Escape From Intimacy*, Ann Wilson Schaef describes her work with addiction. She says, "The addict frequently sees responsibility as accountability and blame, and the relationship, sex or romance addict does not want to be blamed. In recovery we know that to take responsibility means to own one's life."

Don't substitute drugs for the parents you wish you had or the love you didn't receive. Go out and find the love. Love is within you. Begin by loving yourself.

Think about what you would say if God told you, "I want you to be happy for the rest of your life." What would you do to be happy? This is difficult for most adults to answer. If I say to someone: You've graduated from school, you have a scholarship, a fortune has been given to you, what do you want to do?" most adults say, "I don't know."

This question had special meaning for Jeanne Prevo, a woman I saw many years ago. She wrote me to say:

Dear Bernie,

I came to Connecticut to see you in June, 1982. You taught me how to save my life. You gave me hope when I was told there wasn't any hope. You cared for me when I was desperate, bald and very very ill. You called me, wrote to me and gave me the courage to stand up and fight an aggressive war against cancer. And how to win. You showed me the third path. I've had thirteen surgeries since June of 1982, but I am still working as a Special Education teacher. The Board of Education and my Principal kept me employed even when I was in a wheelchair, a walker, used a cane and wore a wig. My class and I worked together in love for each other. Now I have a full head of hair, eyelashes, a new hip, a new colostomy, new silicone fronts and no cancer. I can ride my bike and even dance. Remember when you asked what I would do if God wanted me to be happy for the rest of my life? I didn't know the answer. I've been finding that answer for the last eight years in many ways. Your picture is on my desk for encouragement, your meditation tape is in the recorder, your book on the table, and compassion and love for suffering people in my heart. I passed along your teachings at the hospital to countless people who asked for help. You told me to become real like the Velveteen Rabbit, and Bernie, my joints are loose, I've lost my shape but I am real and alive. God bless.

Note that she wrote, "You **taught me** how to save my life," not "You saved my life." She kept her power.

In *The Velveteen Rabbit*, the Rabbit asks the Skin Horse what it means to be "Real," and the Skin Horse tells him:

> Real isn't how you are made. It's a thing that happens to you. When a child loves you for a long, long time, not just to play with, but REALLY loves you, then you become Real. . . It doesn't happen all at once. You become. It takes a long time. That's why it doesn't often happen to people who break easily, or have sharp edges, or who have to be carefully kept. Generally, by the time you are Real, most of your hair has been loved off, and your eyes drop out and you get loose in the joints and very shabby. But these things don't matter at all, because once you are Real you can't be ugly, except to people who don't understand.

Dealing With Anger

When you are aware of your feelings, one of the strongest you may become aware of is anger. How do you deal with anger when it first comes up, and all through the healing and staying-well process?

There may be a lot of reasons to be angry at the world, but the anger needs to be directed in healthy ways and in a safe environment, so that you can find a healing within.

Anger is a signal. You are being told by your body, your mind, your heart that your territory is being invaded, your sense of self is being trampled on. If you are aware of your anger, you can decide what to do with it. Your immune system may be an internal display of healthy anger, fighting to defend you.

Life is full of difficulties, and the question is how we deal with them. First of all, we need to express our feelings about them. As a computer expert friend says, "Garbage in, garbage out. But garbage out, love can come in." You need to make a place in your life for peace and love, and express the "garbage." How? One way is to put it in a journal. As the psychologist James Pennebaker said in his book *Opening Up*, if you write in a journal about your traumas and your deepest feelings about those traumas, the experience can be a healing one.

Keep a journal. Write down your feelings, day after day. Make notes, so that you remain aware of your feelings. We are incredibly good at suppressing things. But when we do this, the emotions are still inside us, affecting us. I learned that a long time ago. I used to make notes during the day about things I saw in the hospital that were emotional for me. Then at night I couldn't remember what the notes were about. That's how efficient I was at blocking out what was troubling me. And so I began to write more elaborate notes, because I wanted to be able to deal with the feelings. It is important that you take the lid off internally, that you allow your feelings to come up. Otherwise they will be stored up inside, and one day your body will insist that you pay attention to them.

Join a group that is concentrating on the same issues you are facing—whether AA, cancer, AIDS,

Overeaters Anonymous, divorce, well spouses of ill partners or a grieving group. You can talk to the people in the group and share. These people will know what you're going through, and they can discipline you, love you, support you, be tough on you so that you will make the appropriate choices at the appropriate times. It is sometimes difficult to share with family members because in a sense they want to cure the situation. And you have to remind them that if you express anger or fear, you're not asking them to cure everything but to be there to support you physically and emotionally. It might mean giving them a hug so that they feel they've done something for you besides just listen. If they ask how you are, you can say, "I'm a B plus, or a C minus." The rule is that if you're less than a B plus, you always receive a hug. Then they won't feel helpless. They can listen; they can touch; they can support you.

Share your feelings honestly. When people ask, "How are you?" don't automatically smile and say, "Fine." If you **are** fine, wonderful. But suppressing your feelings is destructive. So please, don't put a fixed grin on your face and deny what you are going through and confuse your body. That doesn't constitute positive thinking or true peace of mind.

If you don't express your feelings, particularly anger, you may end up resenting, hating, and becoming a murderer some day, potentially or actually. If you don't express the anger, it will remain inside you, creating depression or even illness, and controlling you. Somehow it will find an outlet—but a destructive outlet.

If someone tells me, "I'm angry at you and your book," I say, "Good," because that person is communicating. I get letters from people who are angry. Many of these are unsigned. That is unfortunate, because then we can't communicate and heal and change each other.

One woman I met told me she threw my book against the wall and that the nurse told her, "Bernie would love that." As she was telling me this story I interrupted her and said, "That's great," and she and I both smiled when she told me what the nurse had said. This is an energy we can work with.

One way of using your energy is through repetitive physical exercise. It can be almost like a meditation. As you are doing rhythmic activity and your body is involved, your thoughts and feelings surface, and then they can be dealt with. It doesn't matter whether you walk, run, swim, dance, garden, or do exercises in a chair if necessary—but try to get your body moving, and you will be amazed at the results.

I meditate regularly every morning when I go out jogging. Thoughts and feelings may come up that I haven't dealt with, and then I can complete the unfinished business. There is a freedom and a knowledge that seem to take over when you get into this state, that help you resolve difficulties. You are more creative.

If you have unexpressed feelings building up during the day, it is important to have a transition period or healing interval before you move into your home life in the evening—a walk home from the train station or from your office, or listening to a tape in the car. You'll need to find some way of decompressing, or your life and family will suffer.

A friend of mine was a bartender. He knew that his job was largely psychotherapy. He saw many people stop on the way home from the office. They were not really there to have a drink; they were there to talk to him. So find someone to talk to. You don't need to use drugs to make you numb, because they don't help you deal with the true issues. When you get home, it's all right to tell the family that you need a moment. When I came home from the hospital and everybody pounced on me to tell me about their exciting or difficult day, many times I couldn't handle it because of what I'd been through myself. It is all right to say, "I need to go into my room, into the den." Close an office door. Do something to and for yourself. Change clothes. Shift gears. Mow the lawn. Clean the house. Get involved in something that makes you lose track of time. That will allow you to reach another state, one in which you are more receptive to those around you.

I have seen music, poetry and art therapists work with people in the hospital so that they can use their energy and anger to create a song or poem or paint a picture. These things have helped heal them, as their pain and feelings came out through these media. Art worked for me when I was in incredible emotional pain as a physician. I learned that I could come home, change into old clothes, go into the room that I had set up in the basement, and paint. The children would gather around me, and we'd all paint together. In a few hours I would be changed by that experience.

People are often told by others how they **should** feel. It is sad when people are so devoid of feeling they think they have to feel what somebody else tells them. I remember the hospice worker who came to a family I was caring for and told them they should be angry, and they weren't. They had dealt with all the issues, and there was nothing to be angry about. But they got angry at the hospice worker, and that made her happy because then she saw anger.

Don't worry about what you're "supposed" to feel, just feel it. Don't judge your feelings; feelings are not to be judged. If you are wondering what to do with them, then the best people to talk to are those who can truly understand you, who have been through the same things and dealt with the same feelings. Where do we find those people? How do we create them?

Finding or Starting a Support Group

There are many ways of finding a support group, including making telephone calls and sending letters to self-help organizations, which will provide you with information about what is going on in your community. Government agencies and volunteer organizations will often connect you with resources. Ask other people with the same problems that you have. Ask your physician.

Take a look at bulletin boards in your community, in health-food stores and in churches and synagogues to see if there is information about the kind of gathering you want.

If you have the passion, you will find what you are looking for. And if no such group exists in your community, start one. It may be as simple as putting an ad in the newspaper or a notice on a bulletin board, asking for others with the same problem who would like to meet and talk to call. But in general you want someone running the meetings who is trained to be what I call "carefrontational"—that is, loving, but confronting you to help you change as a person. You don't want to run a victim group. You can give people a chore to do before they are allowed to enter the group, like reading a book or drawing a picture or filling out a form. It's amazing how many people will decline to do these things, because they don't want to make an effort or are afraid of failing. I have letters from people saying, "I would have joined your cancer groups, but I'm more afraid of art than I am of cancer."

ECaP and other organizations run sessions to help train you if you want to lead groups. Contact them. Generally a health professional is more prepared to do this type of thing, so do try to find one to help you. But if there isn't anybody in your community, then get together with others to do this.

Sit people down in your living room and encourage them to talk to each other. But remember that this is support and discipline. It's support in a way that allows you to take charge of your life and confront your feelings and fears instead of being afraid of the future.

Many groups may not be specific for your affliction, but that can still help you. If we are really trying to help each other, does it matter what the pain is that brings somebody to a meeting? Whether it is cancer, alcoholism, drug addiction, loss of a loved one—many tragedies can bring us together. To some extent our pain can be shared, and we can help each other.

Informal or social groups that you are already a part of can be helpful. We all are afflicted. Share your wound. Sometimes when you tell people what is really going on in your heart, you will be surprised at the support you will receive, and by the deep level at which many people are thinking and feeling in their own private lives. So take a look around you and be aware of what kind of groups you are already a part of, and whether they might be taken to a deeper level.

Sometimes people who have met at one of our workshops or who have shared a hospital room have remained in touch afterward. As one young man pointed out, one of the things our workshops do is to give people permission to really talk to one another intimately and supportively.

I know that appropriate group therapy or individual therapy can prolong survival. I've said, however, that group therapy has more side effects than chemotherapy. What I mean is that it takes courage to change. Being willing to change can be more difficult and stressful than exposing yourself to a variety of chemical or mechanical treatments. Remember, you are opening the lid. Open it in a safe environment. People will help you deal with what comes out, and life will never present you with anything you can't handle.

What we get back to is the fact that if you share your life experience, if you have someone who will listen and are given a chance to express your feelings, then your survival and the quality of your life are also affected.

2
Loving Others: Opening Your Heart

If I can stop one heart from breaking,
I shall not live in vain;
If I can ease one life the aching,
or cool one pain,
or help one fainting robin
Unto his nest again,
I shall not live in vain.

—EMILY DICKINSON

If you want to be happy for an hour
take a nap.
If you want to be happy for a day
go fishing.
If you want to be happy for a month
get married.
If you want to be happy for a year
inherit a fortune.
But if you want to be happy for a lifetime
do something good for someone else.

—WORKSHOP PARTICIPANT (ANONYMOUS)

First Heal the Heart

Susan Duffy is a woman who has been a real teacher and an inspiration for me. I met her twelve years ago when she was given very little hope for long-term survival. She has scleroderma. I didn't know what to do for Susan because in my years as a physician I had never met anyone with a story like hers. Everyone in her family had committed suicide, and she had tried to do so as well. She said she grew up with the message, "Die, kid, die." When I first met her, her rage was incredible. All I could do was listen. I had no solutions.

But as she emptied herself of rage, she began to heal. Over the years she has written me some wonderful letters and taught me some important lessons. In one of her letters she wrote:

> I had only two choices to make, and they were to live or to die. I chose life. It has been painful, working through the issues in my life, but I always

felt the divine hand of God supporting me through it.

I now know that people need to experience the power of love within their own lives. And if you have trouble with God, put the word Love in. That is the mystery of all true healing, the power of love.

The definition of healing for me is one's willingness to become reacquainted with one's own true self and to allow one's fellow man to do the same. This is all done in the power of love and forgiveness. The true essence of love is that it gives, gives and gives with no thought of what it will get back. Because in the end it gets it all back anyway and then some. The healing powers are unconditional love and forgiveness toward oneself and toward others.

I have grown to see so clearly the symbolism of my illness. I hated my family to such a degree that I tried to kill myself, really wanting to kill them. I didn't die that way, but I did get a serious illness. As I grow to understand the true meaning of love, I am learning to understand the powerful impact it has had upon my life. I can see my experience of life as this: I lived in a prison. I had no control of the circumstances which I was born into and I had no control over the parents who raised me. I had no power over the circumstances that I was exposed to. When my prison was so dark that I could not see, and the pain so great that I did not want to see, I heard a knock on the door and had the courage to open it. As I opened the door, in walked love. As love walked in, I then had the power to forgive, I had the ability to accept. As love walked around my prison, it touched every negative item in it, meaning the experiences in my life, and transformed them into something meaningful.

I think the lines of hers that reverberate most strongly for me are:

Heal the heart first. If people can only learn to live in the simplicity of their own heart, they will not only heal themselves, but everyone around them. Heartfelt love is the all time healer. . .

She let love into that dark prison in which she had been trapped, and it changed her and illuminated the darkness. We are capable of making our own weather.

Your Family Motto

As many of you know, my childhood was not like Susan's. I grew up loved. I didn't realize the pain that went on in many other households, and I have realized that this puts me in a minority group. I see in retrospect that my parents were a little like Jungian therapists, without the training.

If someone said to Carl Jung, "Carl, something wonderful has happened," he'd say, "That's too bad, but if we stick together maybe we can get you through this." If the person said, "Something terrible has happened," Jung would reply, "Ah, let's open a bottle of wine. Something good will come of this." That was also the basic message from my mother and father.

From both of my parents I gained a sense of self-worth. I heard my father say nice things about me when I wasn't in the room (and therefore I knew he meant them). When you hear your father say you can be a success in any field, you know he believes in you, and when you go out into the world with that kind of confidence behind you, even though there are conflicts and problems and people won't always like what you do, you know that you are supported. Even if your parents don't like what you are doing, you know that you are loved. That is an enormous difference from the way that most people are brought up, unliked and unloved.

My mother gave me a very simple message. Like Carl Jung, when something disappointing would happen, she would say, "It was meant to be. God is redirecting you, something good will come of this." That may not seem profound, but when you think about it, you realize that nothing can ever go wrong in your life. You can't fail, and God isn't punishing you. God is a resource. You can only be redirected and helped by every event. So even adversity becomes a redirection.

My mother's message allowed me to turn a lot over to God but also to realize that all events are in a sense on my path and meaningful. So I did not go to the college that was my first choice. I didn't do my medical training at the hospital that was my first choice. Many plans I made and things I wanted to do didn't happen. But the places I did go turned out to be the right ones for me. I always had the sense of being on the right path. When we learn that there are redirections and that our intellect doesn't always know the best choices, we open ourselves to some wonderful things.

Jason Gaes, who had cancer at age seven, said, "If God wanted me to be a basketball player, He would have made me seven feet tall. But He gave me cancer, so I'd write a book and help other people." Jason wrote *My Book for Kids with Cansur*. That's what happens when you're loved. Nothing is a punishment.

In a book of his favorite quotes, Norman Vincent Peale says that the message of his mother, Anna Delaney Peale, was "If a door slams shut it means that God is pointing to an open door further on down."

So he grew up with this positive message. But I know there are other families in which the message is that if something good happens, something bad will follow. Or, "You're not smart enough." "We never expected anything of you." "You're too fat." "What a waste your education was." The message is one of a child's being undeserving or ignorant, ugly or guilty. People brought up this way tend to expect difficulties or punishment, not to mention those overtly abused either sexually or psychologically. They don't believe they deserve anything.

What was your family motto? What hypnotic message did your parents pass on to you?

For the first four-and-a-half years of my life I was the only child, and then my sister, Dossie, was born. She is very capable and bright, and we have both always been independent people. We didn't compete with each other. I know I tried to be a good kid because I wanted to contribute something to the family, not because I thought I'd be punished, or because it was demanded of me. I wanted to give something back to my parents for them to be proud of. I had the normal disillusionments and problems, but I also knew that I was loved and so could go on and heal and be healed. As Robert Frost says in his poem "The Death of the Hired Man":

Home is the place where, when you have to go there,
They have to take you in.

That is how I felt about my family—I always knew that they would take me in.

My wife, Bobbie, and I were married in 1954. We have known each other an even longer time, and we'll be together until we get our marriage right.

I gave her a book called *Love* for our 37th anniversary. In it is "The Diary of Adam and Eve," by Mark Twain. Adam and Eve are writing in their journals. The following comes from Adam's journal, and it expresses what I feel about love: ". . . it is better to live outside the Garden with her than inside it without her." And at Eve's grave, "Wheresoever she was, *there* was Eden."

That is how I feel about Bobbie. I know that when she and I are loving, that's what our lives are like. We also describe our marriage as a struggle. Bobbie at workshops has described it as "a long, hard struggle." People sometimes look puzzled at this, because the myth is that if you're in love, you shouldn't have to struggle. Yet after all these years Bobbie and I still hold hands, and people notice that, too.

I was pleased to see that Joseph Campbell described marriage as "an ordeal." I think his words apply to all relationships—with husband, wife, lover, doctor, patient. We are trying to create a third entity, something bigger than the individuals involved. In an interview with Michael Toms in the book *An Open Life*, Campbell said:

> You see the whole thing in marriage is the relation-
> ship and the yielding. Knowing the functions,
> knowing that each is playing a role in an organism.
> One of the things I have realized, and people who
> have been married a long time realize, is that mar-
> riage is not a love affair. A love affair has to do
> with immediate personal satisfaction, but marriage
> is an ordeal. It means yielding, time and again.
> That's why it is a sacrament. You give up your per-
> sonal simplicity to participate in a relationship.
> And when you're giving, you're not giving to the
> other person, you're giving to the relationship. And
> if you realize that you are in the relationship, just
> as the other person is, then it becomes life build-
> ing, a life-fostering and enriching experience. Not
> an impoverishment, because you are giving to
> somebody else. Do you see what I mean? This is
> the challenge of a marriage. What a beautiful thing
> is a life together as growing personalities, each

helping the other to flower rather than just moving into the standard archetype. It's a wonderful moment when people can make the decision to be something quite astonishing and unexpected, rather than cookie mold products.

Life is really a series of marriages, as we touch one another along the way.

In his poem "A Man and a Woman Sit Near Each Other," from his book *Loving a Woman in Two Worlds*, Robert Bly refers to a man and woman breathing for a third body, meaning that the "third body" is the relationship. Like Bly and Campbell, I believe that we create another identity, a third thing, a relationship, which should be life-enhancing and life-fostering and that should allow each person to become his or her unique self. It is a struggle to do that, and doing so leads to conflicts and difficulties, but if the commitment is there, and if the key word, love, is there, then you work at it.

Bobbie and I have raised five children. Our youngest two are twins, and all of the children were born within a seven-year period. So it was an exhausting time, physically and emotionally, when they were young. And I know that we gave them some difficulties—it's hard to give twenty percent of your time to each child. Yet in spite of everything I believe that our children felt safe and secure. I think they know that although we were not and are not the best parents in the world, we love them, and we are still trying to learn. But there was no course for us on parenting. So we say we are sorry and help them to move on, and we continue to love each other.

Bobbie is an only child, and at the time this was written her parents were in their nineties. (Her mother will kill me for telling.) Her father has quite a spirit. Despite deafness and an injury to his spinal cord from a fall many years ago—which means that he cannot control most of his body now or adjust his hearing aid—he still has the will to live and to participate. I admire his determination. I know he teaches our children something, too—that the physical body is not our only reason for being here, and that there are many ways to contribute to the world. (I must share his sense of humor. When I asked him for advice on aging he said, "Remember to fall on something soft." He added, "But I once fell on my wife and broke her leg." His conclusion: "Just fall up!" He died January 23, 1993, after this was written. He tired of his body and left peacefully. He was 97.)

Our children are all grown now, and John Bradshaw says something that I have said to them also: "I'm sorry, forgive me for all the things I didn't know and didn't know how to do." When you have five children, you learn some things by the fourth and fifth child. Our first one, Jonathan, asked years ago, "How come they don't have to do things I had to do?" And my response was, "I've finally learned what is important." Things can be difficult for the first few children.

In a sense I believe none of us really knows our children—what they have lived, their experience of the family—until they are perhaps twenty or thirty and willing to talk to us, and we are willing to listen. They may never be willing to talk, but if they are, we can heal our relationships. If no one is willing to talk, you can keep expressing your love. We all need it. And it will lead to change. Don't ask for it or demand it; give it. It will return.

Our family has had its share of troubles, which have taught Bobbie and me a lot. I think if we listed our troubles, people would know our happiness is a choice, not just a matter of luck.

I think your family is the best teacher. To me family means sharing inadequacies, imperfections and feelings with each other and still loving each other. But even when you set out to love, you may not always be a likable person. And when you're not perfect, forgiveness for yourself and others becomes important. Then you get up the next day and start again. It is a process, like the opening of a bud. It is a flowering, a blooming and blossoming.

Opening to Love: Coming Out of Your Cocoon

If you help a butterfly out of its cocoon, it dies. It has to struggle. All of us—men, women, children—need to struggle to reveal our beauty. At our workshops, both men and women talk about how difficult it is to become open, and especially for men to be open, to express their feelings and emotions. But I don't think one can blame men or society for making men as they are. The differences between men and women aren't all in our training. Some are biological, though their training may teach men to be strong, and brave, and not cry or show feelings.

Men as well as women can in a sense give birth to themselves; they too can go through labor. In workshops I sometimes assign a project to people: "Write a poem about giving birth to yourself." A man named Harold Witt wrote this moving poem:

> Labor? Yes, I guess that's what it is—
> hard work, anyway, to give birth to a person
> out of the insides of the one who was
> instead of only letting the cancer worsen.
>
> Still in the dark, I sense a certain glimmer.
> Push push, and someone new appears
> more insightful, brighter, maybe slimmer
> if not a blonder man of fewer years—

two of me as yet, but one will fade—
that guy who thought that he would live forever—
and out of him this other's being made
not perfect either, but worth all the endeavor.

The truth is that we all need to be balanced human beings, expressing ourselves in a healthy way, opening to all our traits, masculine and feminine. We want men to be caring and to pay attention to feelings, we want women to be assertive, to speak up and express their needs, so that we are all effective, caring human beings.

I've been asked how I became open. I think there is only one reason why people change—because they are in pain, they hurt. They don't like the way they feel, the way they are experiencing life. I chose to struggle against that. Others may choose drugs or suicide when pain occurs.

As I've said, I had a childhood filled with love, and I have a marriage filled with love. But when I became a physician I started to build walls around myself to protect myself from the pain and unhappiness that I was seeing. Yet it was also difficult to seal this pain in, to store it up inside me. This hurt me, my family and my patients. The walled-in city dies. A crack in the wall may save it. Help may enter through the crack.

As a child I had been interested in art; this became a hobby. I went to classes and became proficient at it. Later, as you may know, this art helped restore me. At one point when I was in great pain I used the art as a way of healing. I painted portraits of the family and then painted one of myself. Only later did I realize how sick my portrait was. Think about it. I have asked you to have a portrait done of yourself. You go to the artist, and you put on a cap, mask and gown. Well, that's how I painted myself, in a surgeon's cap, mask and gown. Only my eyes were visible. If you appeared that way before a painter, he or she would say, "But who will know whose portrait this is? I can't see you."

Yes, I was hidden. I had built a wall, and I wasn't even aware of it. I didn't paint anyone else in the family that way. As a matter of fact I had difficulty painting Bobbie, because I wanted her in an evening gown and the painting just wasn't working. One day, after we came home from a bicycle ride and she jumped off her bike (an Elgin from Sears that she has had since she was nine years old) and was straddling it, I said, "Oh, that's you." I painted her standing and holding the handlebars of her bike. That painting was easily done, and it hangs in our living room today, because that was Bobbie. But I couldn't see who I was. Ultimately I began to resist the hiding; it was too painful. Yet the pain we see as an enemy ultimately cracks the walls and saves the one who resides behind them.

There is a story about a man who was asked why he didn't react to the death of his wife, and he said that he just decided not to show his pain. We need to see that that is another kind of death as well. This is what I see in many physicians. They have died inside, and they have put up walls around themselves for protection. No feelings are being expressed, but the feelings are in there. I knew from my family that this was not an appropriate way to live, and that the walls don't really protect you—they kill you.

So my pain changed me. That's what led me to want to love more, that's what brought me to this path. When I look at a room full of faces, I feel as though I know everyone's life story. When we go to a workshop and we have 150 people introduce themselves, it is an extraordinarily moving experience. Many people say that this is the most important part of the workshop: Just in sharing our pain and realizing our ability to survive, we gain strength from each other.

I remember a rabbi saying that if God were light and love and were all alone out there, He would be very lonely. So you need mirrors to reflect and spread that love, and people are those mirrors. That's our job, to keep reflecting that light and love, out of free choice. What makes it meaningful is free will. This also makes life dangerous, because people make choices that can be painful and destructive. But without choices, love would be meaningless. I think this is why Adam and Eve left the Garden, to show that the love that exists by choice is more meaningful and healing than anything else.

Unconditional Love

I once received a letter from a man who asked how he could achieve unconditional love, especially when people might not give it in return. I had to laugh at this question, because "unconditional" means that you don't have to receive anything in return for what you give. As Elisabeth Kübler-Ross said, "It's giving with no expectations." That is probably the simplest definition of unconditional love.

If you are giving love and are not expecting anything in return, then you truly have something. When you do something special for someone else, you don't need everybody in the neighborhood applauding you. You are rewarded by the act. The poem by Emily Dickinson quoted at the beginning of this chapter says it beautifully.

Have you ever rescued a bird and had it fly off again? With all of our children and our interest in animals, many a veterinarian has used our home as a place for animals to recover. Our children have always brought home wounded creatures, particularly birds. I can remember one that had flown into a store window. Bobbie and I brought it home. Bobbie revived it, and two days later it flew off. Our daughter Carolyn once brought home a pigeon named Louis (don't ask how

she knew that that was its name), and he was with us
for several weeks. He lived in the front yard, coming
down for breakfast each day, and finally flew off. You
feel that you have accomplished something. The bird
and its family do not have to thank you or send a gift
every year. You are rewarded by saving a life. The
reward is contained in what you did, an act of love.

When we are giving love, we are beautiful. I know
a school counselor who tells the students that there are
no ugly children, and they think he is crazy. But they
begin to understand that he means when they are giving love, they are beautiful. I know many stories about
patients who are beautiful no matter how distressing it
may be to look at them in a physical sense.

There was a lady in the hospital who was paralyzed—she was in an iron lung. She still managed to
have a birthday card for every nurse who took care of
her. Nobody figured out how she knew their birthdays,
or how she got people to provide cards for everybody,
but she did. She was beautiful.

If you are going to judge and weigh other people's
responses, you are setting yourself up for conditional
love. If you give two hours of your time to someone
who gives you back only an hour, you may resent them.
I see people dying who say, "I never got back what I
gave out." I don't think they really loved; they were
measuring everything. So don't measure, just give, and
watch what happens. Because that's the greatest gift of
love. It is reflected back to you by all the people
around you.

In his book *The Direction of Human Development*,
Ashley Montagu says:

Love implies the possession of a feeling of deep
involvement in another, and to love means to communicate that feeling of involvement to him. Love

is unconditional, it makes no bargains and it trades with no one for anything. Love is supportive. Love is firm. Love is most needed by the human organism from the moment of birth. Love is reciprocal in its effect and is as beneficial to the giver as it is to the recipient. Love is creative. Love enlarges the capacities of those who are loved. . .

Love is tender.

Love is joyful.

Love is fearless.

Love enables the person to treat life as an art.

Love as an attitude of mind and as a form of behavior is adaptively the best and most efficient of all adjustive processes in enabling the human being to adapt himself to his environment.

For the person and the species love is the form of behavior having the highest survival value.

Ashley Montagu also helped me when he said that when you are having difficulty with a person, "act as if you love them." By making that choice—this does not imply a deception, but a choice to love—I have helped myself and my relationships. This is what I try to share with people over and over again—that love heals. It may not cure every problem, but it can heal every life.

The Support Person and Caregiver

When we give love, it sustains the one who gives it as well as the one who receives it. We cannot cure our loved ones or take away all of their problems, but we can support them with our love. The important thing for the support person to remember is to give your husband, wife, lover, child—whomever—love. And to listen, but to also let them have their disease. It is their disease, so don't create guilt with questions like, "Did you meditate? Eat your vegetables? Take your medicine?" If they hear this all the time, they won't want to listen to you. You can gather information and give them resource materials, but if they throw the materials out, that's their choice. You don't want them to throw you out. If they have your love, they will find their path. You must give them permission to find their path, even if it differs from what you would like them to do. So give them the resources, but don't give them the sermon.

It is also important to find your own support and to do the things that we recommend to the person who is ill. We are all mortal. Eat a proper diet, meditate, exercise, get a massage, keep a journal, form a group. What I'm really saying is that if you're alive, these things are good for you. Most of all, try to find support and therapy so that you can express your feelings and difficulties in a healthy way, rather than attacking the ill person. Whether you feel anger at your loved one, at God, or at someone else, express those feelings in a safe, appropriate way.

A friend who has become very special to me is Anita Tejedat. We met at a workshop and have kept in touch. Her husband is ill. She has the habit of waking up in the middle of the night and writing down her thoughts, or I should say letting them be written down. One piece she sent me was called "How About Me." In it she wrote:

> What about the person who is not the one with the illness? Yes, how about me? How am I doing? No one ever seems to ask. A selfish thought when I am not the one who has the disease. No, my pain doesn't have a medical label, my fear is abstract, there isn't any medicine that can take it away. It is the pain of sharing my life, my love, my hopes, my dreams, my future with someone whose life seems to be shattered and all those things stolen from

him. How am I doing? Well, since you asked, I'm scared shitless. I'm scared to love all the way now, because the loss is too great. I'm scared because I'm real angry and I want to scream out to God, "Are you nuts?" Or to my beloved who is sick, "Snap out of it and make it go away," or to friends and family who have become distraught over trivialities, "Shut the hell up, you don't know how lucky you are." I'm scared because my own life and love, and hopes and dreams and future are so connected to my love's that I wonder what will become of me. I'm scared because I see and live the reality of what is and still reach for the idealism I've always had and wonder if I'm fooling myself. Maybe you could say a prayer of courage for me, so I can continue on and care.

I believe that at a deep level, Anita knows the answers. She wrote another letter, one morning at dawn:

When someone you love is falling apart with the dreaded disease that seems to be consuming him little by little, you become steeped in fear and anger and denial and often feel helpless. What can you do? What is the purpose of all this? "Why, dear God, why?" is the question that goes around and around in your head. You've heard it said that when you have your health you have everything. I wonder about that. Do you really? My beloved husband is sick. I live and feel and breathe these things and live with the questions always. But I have found one of the answers. I give it to you. No it is not true that when you have your health you have everything. What is true is, if you have someone who truly cares about you, when you do not have your health, you have everything. It is easier to buy good health than to buy good love. No amount of money can do that. Love is a free gift. It can give us all the strength we need to go on when there ain't no more to give. . . Screaming out in the quiet, "I adore you. I hate this. I am here. If only my love could heal you, you would be healed instantly. Together we'll get through this. We'll beat this thing." And in my heart I know our love is better than anything else, richer than anything else, healthier than anything else, and will rise above anything else, yes, and can even heal. No, when you have your health you do not have everything, but when you have a heart, a soul, connected to yours, be it wife, husband, child, friend, lover, parent, sister, brother, doctor, nurse, whoever, that says, "I love you, I'm here," you have everything.

I don't know any way to say that better. We need to care for each other, to love, and to be there for each other.

Anita has now begun doing workshops for family members and support persons of people with serious illnesses. We all need to learn how to keep the disease from spreading to our relationships.

Another person who has used her pain as a resource is Maggie Strong. She has written a wonderful book called *Mainstay*, about the family side of chronic illness, and about her anger, fatigue, fear and her struggle to keep herself and her husband and two children afloat during her husband's illness. She describes how she learned to accept love and help from friends and family, and how she learned to give back some of the responsibility to her husband. She writes in *Mainstay*:

To become chronically ill is to lose yourself as a healthy person: you grieve. To be married to someone ill and to watch a man or woman you love suffer means you mourn. You mourn the lost marriage, the lost family, the suffering of the mate, and your lost self—the one who could feel dependent, who could ask to be indulged, the lighthearted you. And often with chronic illness you mourn a lost or reduced sexuality.

Because she felt so desperately alone, she has started an organization called the Well Spouse Foundation for others in her situation.

As the "healthy" caregiver you must find ways to take time for yourself, so that you don't have to get sick in order to restore yourself and have some freedom. What will the family disease do to the children if you don't create a healthy example and show them how to deal with afflictions and adversity? Remember that our attitudes toward life are passed on to our children. There are psychological genetics too.

Raising Healthy Children

I have heard a lot of talk about the "damage" that people's parents have done to them, and a lot of concern from people that they not pass this on to their own children. First of all, I don't blame parents, because they had parents. And if we place blame, we don't get anywhere. Once damage is done to you, however, you are the one who has to undo it. This is your responsibility. It will include grieving, a time to mourn and be angry. I know that the physical and psychological abuse that some people have received has been horrendous, but you can heal. You can free yourself of this pain. You are the solution; that is the second point to understand.

When Keith was angry at me for not being the father he felt he needed, I told him, "Picture me as an alcoholic lying on the sofa, drunk. Are you going to remain unhappy and blame me or are you going to say,

'Well, he's no help, I've got to do something myself'?"
Understand that you are responsible for healing and
for changing, and literally when you heal, you are likely
to heal your parents and your whole family. Because
you will shift into a place where you can understand,
forgive and love. Keith has done all that for us.

I'm not saying that I'm perfect at raising children. I
would have been better at it if I had had a training
course in addition to the thirty years of bringing them
up. And that's why grandparents are often better at this
than parents. They've had the experience—the training
course—and they are better with the second group.

When you have a child, make sure that child knows
that you are imperfect. Don't be afraid to share your
inadequacies and emotions. Let children know that it is
all right to get angry at you, and let them feel safe
doing so. They will still love you and heal you. Once
when our son Jeffrey was a little pipsqueak and had
driven me crazy, I chased him around the kitchen,
grabbed him and was about to wallop his behind when
he said, "You can't hit me." I said, "Why not?" And he
said, "Because I'm a person. And if you hit me I'll call
the police." That beautiful truth led me to let go, laugh
and love him even more. After that I never spanked
any of our children again.

Listen to your child. Verbalize your love, show
your love. Let your child know that he or she is loved,
regardless. In other words, loved unconditionally.
Make it clear that he or she doesn't have to be perfect
in the sense of physical appearance or school grades.
Adopting this attitude doesn't mean that you don't discipline your child or that you like everything he or she
does. But you can talk about these things. If you have
never been loved, this will be hard work for you and
for your children.

I recently viewed a videotape of therapist Gary
Smalley. He shows the audience a Stradivarius violin
and they are in awe of it.

I often hold up infants, or show photographs of infants, at my workshops and people react as if they are seeing a Stradivarius.

What happens as we grow up? The awe, wonder, potential and honor are lost.

Please continue to look at your children as valuable treasures. Honor them and yourself.

A child must know certain necessary rules in our society. With love and discipline comes a healthy child, one who can meet his or her needs in an appropriate way and who doesn't need the addictions that we see today in so many of our children—or the suicides, self-destructive and pathological behavior. I believe that all of those stem from the lack of love and support that a family can provide. If children don't receive healthy love they search for a love they can control; they develop addictions to gain what wasn't available from parents, and sometimes children even commit suicide instead of killing their unhealthy parts and becoming new people.

Even if you don't have children of your own, you can help children to become healthier. When my sister and I were discussing what to put on my father's headstone, I was impressed as I jogged through a cemetery on Cape Cod with the fact that people had recorded on tombstones the number of years, months and days that someone had lived. And I thought how important those moments must have been to those people. But my sister thought that emphasized time too much, and she wanted my father's headstone to say, "Husband, father, grandfather, great-grandfather." To me, that emphasized the relationship aspect too much. I think people could spend a lifetime here, and whether or not they had children was not the significant event. The world could have been their child.

I am very aware now of the pain and abuse that many children go through, because I speak at grade schools, junior and senior high schools and colleges.

Few of the children seem to believe that their parents really love them or would protect or stand up for them. Many of them are feeling like failures. Some (30% in certain studies) have seriously thought about suicide. Part of the reason I go to the schools is to let the students know that somebody cares. I hope that you will think about getting to know more young people. Speak to them—tell them about yourself and your life. What you say is not the most significant thing; what is significant is that you are talking to them, sharing with them. That means they're worth something.

In one of my favorite books, *The Human Comedy* by William Saroyan, a teacher speaks to her students. What she says reminds me so much of my parents:

> I am eager for my boys and girls to exert themselves, to do good and to grow nobly. What my children appear to be on the surface is no matter to me. I am fooled neither by gracious manners nor by bad manners. I am interested in what is truly beneath each kind of manners. If the children of my classroom are human, I do not want them to be alike in the manner of being human. If they are not corrupt, it does not matter to me how they differ from one another. I want each of my children to be himself. I want my children to be people, each one separate, each one special, each one a pleasant and exciting variation of all the others. I wanted him to know that each of you would begin to be truly human when, in spite of your natural dislike of one another, you still respect one another. That is what it means to be civilized. Before you go very far along in the world, you will hear laughter many times and not the laughter of men alone, but the mocking laughter of things themselves seeking to embarrass and hold you back. But I know you will pay no attention to that laughter.

This teacher gave her students a great gift—the knowledge that they could go on, through any laughter or criticism, knowing they had been loved.

All children are lovable. Try to keep that sense of "lovableness" alive within your own children and yourself. Allow them to express themselves. Keep their baby pictures out on view, on your office desk and at home, on tabletops or on the walls, so that they will see these and know that they are loved and valued. (Include your own baby pictures too.) Our living room at home is filled with things the children have made over the years. We displayed these when they were in grade school, and they are still sitting there twenty years later. Let your children know that they are creative and wonderful creatures.

Susan Duffy's parents never took a photograph of her. They were real estate agents. They took pictures of the houses. She has no physical evidence of herself as a lovable child. When you grow up with messages that say, "You are beautiful and lovable," it is much easier to become the adult who can reach out, take a chance and even get hurt.

Several years ago when I was in Boulder, Colorado, I met some people who had formed a group to combat child abuse. They gave me a paper called "Psycho History in Action," written by Robert McPharland and Kathleen Linden. "Psycho History" is based on the belief that when methods of raising children are changed, historic changes can result in society. In 1983, after a three-year-old boy was murdered by his mother and her boyfriend, one of the group initiated public discussion to develop a communitywide program to prevent child abuse.

All parents need help when a child is born. All parents feel like hitting their children on some occasions. But child abuse is preventable. I believe we can take a lot more action to prevent it by sharing our feelings and expressing them, so that we don't become the abusers. Knowing we are capable of abuse is the first step in not carrying it out. We have to look at our dark side, our shadow, at all the parts of ourselves that we might not like. And then we are consciously aware of them and don't have to act them out.

It may sound silly, but I wish we could license parents. Perhaps when a child is conceived, the two future parents would be assigned to a group in which they could share their feelings. We could insist that they attend as part of their medical care, just as we insist on many other things in society. And so we would have groups of parents, therapists, grandparents coming together. We might start when people are in high school, or even earlier. Delivery of the baby, care of the baby, would be part of the discussion. After the birth of the child, perhaps for a year or two or three, the mother and father would continue to be part of a group of other parents, grandparents and therapists so that they could share their frustrations and their pain.

Parenting then wouldn't lead to child abuse in difficult times; instead, parents would express their anger and other feelings within the group and receive love back. They would learn that anger can be appropriately expressed. When feelings can be expressed in a healthy way, we don't blame our children. And when a group is made up of people with a common concern, be it cancer, AIDS, quadriplegia or parenthood, we all know each other's troubles and can discipline each other and help find ways to heal our lives. Abuse need not continually be passed on. We could also train people in how to talk to children so that the children aren't made to feel inadequate, and they can ultimately become healthy parents themselves.

I know that as a father there were times I felt guilty because my judgment was not always correct. If one of the children said, "My leg hurts," I might tell him or her to take a hot bath, but maybe the child had something that a bath was not going to help. Every time a child has a leg pain, your first thought is not osteogenic sarcoma, but that the child might have fallen and bumped him- or herself or strained a muscle. We all feel guilty at times, but this can be healthy guilt if we go on to ask, "What can I do now? How can I bring in love? How can I help my child rather than persecute myself and the child? How can something good come of this?" Healthy and loving people do not bury themselves in guilt, fault, blame and shame. They move on.

3
Healing Yourself: A Do-It-Yourself Kit for Getting Well

The great events of world history are at bottom, profoundly unimportant. In the last analysis, the essential thing is the life of the individual. This alone makes history; here alone do the great transformations take place. . . in our most private and most subjective lives we are not only the passive witnesses of our age, and its sufferers, but also its makers.

—CARL JUNG
CIVILIZATION IN TRANSITION

"The New Day"

Once when I was speaking in Toronto I met a wonderful woman named Fay Finkelstein. She had always been a fighter, fighting odds, fighting statistics. When she developed cancer of the liver, she fought that too. She wrote a letter to a woman in Sweden who also had liver cancer. I want to quote from that letter, because it says so much about loving and living and being well. Fay wrote:

> Hi, I'm writing at the request of Dr. Bernie Siegel and your brother's fiancee. I'm also writing to you because I want to. I understand that you have liver cancer. I was told over a year ago that I would probably die within six weeks. I didn't die. I don't plan to die for a long time. The advice I can offer you is what worked for me.
>
> "*One*, don't believe anyone who tells you when you will die. *Two*, nobody knows when another

person will die. *Three*, liver cancer does not mean death, necessarily. *Four*, if you want to live, fight for it. *Five*, get away from anyone who does not support whatever action you decide to take for yourself, and that even includes family. *Six*, find something, anything, that you truly love to do and throw yourself completely into this activity. It will become a form of meditation for you. It will take your mind off your illness and allow your body to heal itself. *Seven*, if the doctor offers you a treatment and you believe in it, do it. *Eight*, believe in yourself. *Nine*, death is not failure. Everyone dies. Just give life your best shot. I have been on different forms of chemotherapy for over two years. The drugs I believed in worked, the drugs I didn't like not only didn't work, but the tumors grew.

In a workshop Fay had heard me tell a story about the lawyer who had really wanted to be a violinist but didn't become one because of his parents. When he learned he had a brain tumor and was told he had only a year to live, he quit his law practice and took out his violin. A year later he was playing in an orchestra with no sign of his brain tumor. Fay said that when she heard this, "I hit my husband with my elbow and said, 'We're buying a piano on the way home.'" She also made him get her a keyboard when she went for a bone marrow transplant, one she could take into the unit with her. Her letter continues:

I love making music. I play the piano two hours a day. It has been my meditation. I've gotten rid of many stresses in my life. I don't refuse help from anyone who truly wants to help me. I even ask for help when I feel the need. I don't deal with false pride anymore. Pride is loving yourself, and I love myself no matter how I look or feel. Do what feels good to you. Don't let people tell you to either live or die—you decide. It really is not the years that we are here on earth, it is what we do with the time we have. I may live two more weeks or two more years or I may live to be an old lady. Whatever time I have, I am enjoying my life.

In the kitchen of our Cape Cod home is a needle-point by Fay entitled "The New Day":

This is the beginning of a new day.
God has given me this day to use as I will.
I can waste it; or use it for good.
What I do is important because
I'm exchanging a day of my life for it.
I want it to be—
    Gain, not loss;
    Good, not evil;
    Success, not failure;
in order that I shall not regret
the price I have paid for it.

One of the most important relationships that will come up in your life, as Fay learned, is with your physician. She helped hers to see her as a survivor, not as a statistic.

Finding a Doctor to Join Your Team

I met an oncologist—Dr. Salvatore Scialla, of Scranton, Pennsylvania—who said, "I see my relationship with my patient as a marriage." That's the kind of doctor you want. I've heard his patients say, "He doesn't take my power away. I feel safe in his office." That's what you want to feel, two people forming a bond that has a life of its own.

I use the key word **relationship** to suggest that you and the physician are together in a difficult time, and that you are going to approach the difficulties together. There is a commitment on both sides. Each person is interested not just in him- or herself, but in life-enhancing, life-fostering behavior that allows you to be a unique individual who fights for your life. It is not just an issue of your disease, but of what you experience as a whole person, and whether you are supported and attended to by the physician. Remember that the doctor's title is "attending physician."

It is your life, not the doctor's. The doctor doesn't necessarily have to agree with everything you are doing. There may be some conflict between you, but that is still communication. Difficulties are something you can discuss and work out. You are like "war buddies" fighting a common enemy. You both make a commitment to the relationship—not to what each individual does or to the treatment, but to the relationship. I like the term **war buddies** because it suggests that although there can be conflict between you, you are fighting together as a team. And in a sense even the war can be a form of communication.

When you go to see a doctor you are usually feeling vulnerable, and the doctor can seem to have great power. But in your work together you have to be your unique self. Don't be intimidated.

I know some patients who have sat down and been totally sincere with the doctor, and this sincerity has led to tears and hugs on the part of both of them. If you initiate such sincerity and closeness and there is no response and you don't sense there is a human being on the other side of the desk, get up and get out.

Some people may feel, "But I can't get out. I am in a health plan." Then let me tell you what one woman did. She showed up at her health facility with her lawyer beside her, sat down in front of the doctor, and said, "You and I do not have a good relationship. It is destructive for me when I am trying to battle cancer.

I'm going to get another doctor, and the health plan will continue to pay. My lawyer is here to work that out." She got up and left. I met her at an oncology conference where she spoke to oncologists about survival. Don't be afraid to change your doctor (or to use his or her first name).

One of the things I've always told our children is that if they are traveling and they have an injury or an illness and go to an emergency room, they should ask the E.R. nurses who they would have take care of them if they had the same problem. You could also do this by calling the oncology floor, or the nurse on cardiology. You will hear from the nurses about someone who is capable and caring.

When that won't work, how do you find a doctor? You'll have to do some scouting. Ask questions. People have sat in doctors' waiting rooms and sensed what these felt like and what the staff was like. You can interview a doctor, make an appointment to talk to him or her. Sometimes the doctor may just be too busy; if he or she doesn't initially have time to sit and listen, you can express yourself through a letter.

One woman said she just asked her doctor, "Do you believe in me?" Ask that kind of question. Ask if the doctor will respect you and your ideas. You are living your unique situation, and you want to know that the doctor will take care of you and not just treat your disease.

A concept that has been of incredible importance to me is that of the "native" and the "tourist." What you want is to find a doctor who understands what it is to be a "native." In his book *Patient Encounters: The Experience of Disease*, James Buchanan writes of how the doctor is like a traveler in a foreign country:

This whole business of dying is so completely misunderstood by the living. The assorted visitors, well-wishers, bereaved family members, curious doctors, distracted nurses, angry attendants, that one receives throughout the day are like travelers in a foreign country. They enter the court and kingdom of the patient but only on official business of import and export; they tarry not, nor do they adopt the local customs of the country within which they find themselves. Indeed there is an arrogance, even an insolence to these tourists which is the insulation by which they protect themselves against the contamination of death. After all, what do they know of pain, sweat and incontinence, putrefaction of rotting flesh and the sheer humiliation of not being able to control your bladder and bowels? They measure your fever but they do not suffer it. They study your blood but they do not bleed it. They palpate your liver, your spleen, your guts; but they do not feel them. They hear your heart and yet cannot feel its weakened beat; they measure your blood pressure and yet cannot feel its intensity; they peer with curious abandon into the various interstices, holes, canyons, craters of your body and yet are never part of the great cavern you have become. They are guests, not residents, of this house of death which you inhabit. How then could they possibly understand?

It is only the native who experiences the disease, and the disease is always unique to that native. So be sure your experience is cared for by the doctor and your unique needs are met. The doctor is just not treating the disease mechanically. In my work I have found that we all have great potential, but only a minority of us are willing and unafraid to be exceptional and express our uniqueness.

Exceptional Patients: The Willingness to Be Inspired

What does it mean to be an exceptional patient? I think back to that time fifteen years ago when Bobbie labeled the first people who came to our group meetings "exceptional cancer patients." They had certain characteristics, one of which was that they were willing to make choices. They reached out and took chances. I don't mean that they took undue risks or chances with their lives, but chances related to living. I like to think of it as the willingness to be inspired. They were ready to experience new things, whether it meant floating in a hot tub, eating vegetables, getting a massage, or trying a whole host of therapies. They chose what was right for them at that moment. If it didn't work, they let go of it. If it did provide them with something, they would continue. They didn't run to other people and say, "Decide what to do with my life." They learned from others but didn't let others decide for them.

Exceptional patients take responsibility. They are not afraid of failure; they focus on their abilities. They don't say, "If I don't do this right and cure myself, I've failed." They see that "F" is for "Feedback," not "Failure." (Notice that the difference between the words **ordinary** and **extraordinary** is **extra**.) None of us can live forever, and yet I do think of exceptional patients as survivors.

Once when I was in Colorado I met a young woman who said, "I stopped using dental floss and wearing a seat belt when I was told I was going to be dead in six months. Then I began to re-floss my teeth and put on a seat belt, and I knew there was something in me choosing life again." She underwent surgery and chemotherapy to fight for her life. As her hair fell out she saved it, put it in a basket, gave it a name and made it her pet. Her friends said, "That's disgusting."

But I laughed and told her it was wonderful. That is survival behavior, and she is alive and well today.

One quality I've noticed that survivors always seem to have is a sense of humor, even in the midst of adversity. One lady wore a different rubber animal nose when she went to see her doctor each week. The third week, she said, "My doctor noticed, and smiled." Another lady wore a belly dancer's costume; another, a surgical outfit. One wore an army uniform so that she would feel more assertive, and another wore a sweatshirt saying "Hugs are good for you." She chased her doctor around his office; he now accepts hugs. Doctors can begin to have a sense of humor too. As one doctor said when he was poking around with a needle to inject chemotherapy into a lady's portacath, "Don't worry, I'll find it if it kills you." Henny Youngman tells a story about a doctor who said to a man, "You have six months to live." When the man replied, "I can't pay your bill within six months," the doctor said, "Well, I'll give you another six months then." And the laughter helped heal both of them.

One woman brought her physician a humorous birthday card. He enjoyed it very much, and the next week when she came for chemotherapy, he said, "Where's my card?" She explained, "That was for your birthday." He said, "But it helped me get through the week. I want a humorous card every week." Later she told me, "It took me a while to realize what he did for me. I spend half an hour a week in the drugstore picking out a humorous card for him, chuckling and enjoying myself."

This is a wonderful lady, with a sense of humor. She said, "I was told that I would die at Christmastime. But I said, 'No, I won't!' The doctor asked, 'How can you be so sure?' I said, 'I work in K mart. We're so busy that **nobody** dies in K mart at Christmas.'" And that helped her survive. When she was complaining about draggin' around her chemotherapy pump I told her, "You're just the dragon lady." And she smiled and became The Dragon Lady and used the dragons in her imagery to help fight her disease.

Are you capable of being exceptional? Absolutely. What does that mean? It means participating and understanding: "I have a role here. I'm not the submissive sufferer that the word **patient** implies, willing to undergo everything without speaking up, or raising a little hell, maybe even getting words like **interfering**, **uncooperative** or **difficult** in my medical record."

If you are called "the character" by the hospital staff, it may be because you've asked questions and are behaving like an individual—whether this means not wearing hospital garb, or asking lots of questions, or rarely being in your room. You are seen as difficult, but that's survival behavior. It doesn't actually mean creating conflict or adversaries.

One woman wrote and said that she had trained her medical resident to obediently knock at the door and not disturb her if she was on what she called her "love line," meaning a long-distance call to her family. She taught her oncologist to sit down and look her in the eye instead of walking out while saying, "Any questions?" She questioned nurses about any treatment she didn't understand. She was fortunate enough to have good nurses respond to and respect her. Rather than belittling her, they gave her power. She certified only two phlebotomists to touch her one functioning vein and anyone who wanted to examine her had to "pay" by hugging her or rubbing her "lucky" bald head.

A friend got the word **character** in his medical record. He had his fax machine and his computer brought to his hospital transplant room, and the hospital staff began to refer to him not by his name but by the term **character**. But he healed twice as quickly as anyone expected. He said, "One day I heard the doctor in the hallway tell my wife, 'You know what your husband needs transplanted? His brain.'" Now at that hospital they are teaching other people to be "characters." It is important to be a unique person and not just the **patient** or your diagnosis.

Arthur W. Frank in his book *At the Will of the Body: Reflections on Illness* tells how while he was out of his hospital room a sign saying "Lymphoma" was put on the door. What would you do if you found that on your door? If I saw that—whether the label was "myocardial infarction" or "melanoma" or "colon cancer," I would tear it off and write, "Human being in here," and beneath that, "If you're looking for a lymphoma, go to the pathology department."

Being exceptional also means saying, "I want to learn about myself; I want to challenge myself; I want to change."

Know that you are capable of being inspired and of achieving what others have achieved and sometimes what no one else has ever achieved. It takes a lot of courage to be the first. I've seen that when people ask, "Has anyone ever been cured of my disease?" I'll always remember the lady who asked that question. I said, "If you were in a concentration camp would you ask, 'Does anyone ever get out of here?'" And she told me, "I survived the concentration camp." I think that question saved her life. Because then she found strength inside herself to draw on.

A woman who had epilepsy and seizures for years was given more and more anticonvulsive medication by her doctor. She went for further opinions and finally started an epilepsy control class, realizing it was time for her to take control of herself. She persisted in asking the doctors for tests, and indeed the tests revealed that as she had suspected, she had a tumor. She believed that her seizures would cease after the tumor was removed. So she had it taken out; it was benign, and after the surgery she had no further seizures. She wrote me to say "thank you."

I also received a letter from a lady with epilepsy who was mad at me for making her feel guilty. Same material and disease. Why two different responses? I think it's because the first woman took charge and knew something; the second felt that participation and responsibility mean blame.

Another woman told me that several years ago she noticed an enlarged lymph node in her neck. She went to at least five doctors because the first ones all said, "It's nothing." The fifth one took it out, and it was a lymphoma. She kept her power.

I know a young woman who developed a breast mass and was told, "You're too young to have cancer." Ultimately when she was graduated from college and went for a pre-employment physical, the doctors were astounded by the mass in her breast and wondered why she hadn't taken care of herself. She told them, "The doctor said I'm too young to have cancer." She died of breast cancer, furious at the doctor and upset with herself, and I think that all that rage and resentment hastened her demise. I tried to get her to write a letter to that doctor, hoping that he could say, "I will never let this happen again," so that out of her pain, something good might come. A malpractice suit does not heal the rage and resentment.

If you ever have an intuitive inner knowing, don't accept anyone else's opinion. Pursue yours. There have been people I've seen in the office who have a breast lump that has been unchanged for years; the mammograms are the same; but one day they'll come in and say, "There's something different. It needs to be removed." I know that they have an inner awareness, and I certainly listen to them and think that what they say is as valid as any lab test.

The key to unique individuals is: They keep their power.

Knowing the Right Treatment

It is you we are treating, not just a disease. The right treatment is what is right for you at the moment. That might in some cases even mean stopping therapy or having no treatment at all. Michael Lidington, a young man I'll say more about later, had his cancer come back (We'll discuss his poem later on pp. 121). He told his mother, "I'm not going for further therapy, I'm going to camp." For two weeks he went to a camp for children with cancer. That was his therapy, his right choice and his family could accept it.

What are you willing to continue to do? At times it may be to have aggressive therapy. I heard one man say, "I'm going through this because I want to fight for my life, but my brother, who is a doctor, wonders why I'm doing it." Well, that is his choice. He was doing it because it felt right to him. He wanted to live to see his son grow up.

You can say, "This is my life, and I don't want to go through with this therapy. It isn't appropriate for me. I don't want to go through something that has these side effects and alters my life." You may want to eat only vegetables, or pray, or even say that it is time for you to go.

A beautiful young man named David Puskaric was taken by his friends to a cemetery after he developed cancer. They told him, "We don't want you here." His family told him there were four good reasons why he shouldn't die, meaning all of them as well as himself. And then he wrote a poem called "The Year of Despair," which includes these lines:

My family and friends say for them they want
    me to fight.
In my opinion what gives them the right.
I see death as an end to my suffering and pain
But why can't my friends and family see the
    same gain?

Doctors, nurses, family and friends make chemo
    sound like a big hug
So why don't they lie here and get that nasty drug?

79

HEALING
YOURSELF

I told David when I first met him to suggest that
his friends have a bone-marrow transplant with him,
and his friends began to understand and ease up. I suggested he explain to his family that one of the four reasons was appropriate—that he was to go through therapy to save his life so that he could continue to love
them, but that you do not go through those things for
your father, mother and sister. And they began to
change and understand, and they were the ones who
mailed me his poem.

It is your life, and you have a right to say no. You
have a right to sixteen doctors' opinions. You don't
have to do what they say. If like most people you cher-
ish living, you will want to participate in every way you
can—medical and otherwise—to help yourself. It may
mean becoming more spiritual, it may mean that your
family and your doctor and you all come together to
use every available resource.

A student sent me a copy of a painting called "The
Consultation," by Harry Anderson. It shows a patient
in bed, with a nurse standing with medication, a physician on the other side of the bed thinking and a spiritual figure at the head of the bed touching the patient.
Use everything in that painting: you, the doctor, the
nurse, your spiritual faith, medications and all available treatments.

The right treatment is not purely about your disease. You decide—don't feel that you have to do what
others tell you to do. Otherwise, what I worry about is
that you'll pursue a certain regimen and have so many
side effects that your family and doctor will say, "Oh,
this is too much for you, we'd better stop." Then you
can sit back and smile and say "Good." If that's how
you feel, don't have the treatment in the first place. I'm

not trying to get people to refuse treatment, but it is something to discuss, so that you can keep your power. If you're going to go through labor pains to produce a result, let it be your choice.

How do you know the right treatment? For me there are many factors, including your intuition. You could draw a picture of yourself in the operating room, receiving chemotherapy or having radiation. Or draw yourself eating certain foods. Sometimes a picture will show that a particular diet is a burden. One man drew a picture showing the kitchen of his home with everyone standing on his or her head. I asked, "Why is everyone upside down?" He said, "I'm eating a macrobiotic diet to cure my cancer, but I hate macrobiotics, my wife doesn't like preparing it, and the kids won't show up for meals." He said, "I prefer to have chemotherapy." All right, then go ahead and do it.

I'll say more about dreams later, but it is clear that when it comes to choices about therapy, they can help us. What are your dreams? Write them down. A woman who was trying to decide whether or not to have chemotherapy wrote to me about a dream in which her dead son appeared. She dreamed she was staying in a large, dark, old hotel with her husband; then, suddenly, she found herself in a newer part of the same building with her son, who had died of a malignant tumor many years before. He was showing her around. It was lovely and very light. They walked up an open staircase. She thought she should be staying in this new part of the hotel. Then she thought of her husband and somehow knew that he wouldn't be in the new place with her. Her son disappeared, and she found herself outside the old building not knowing how to find her husband. Then she woke up, and the message was clear: She chose chemotherapy. She chose what she felt would give her life.

Another lady dreamed that she was in a building in which there was an elevator and a staircase, and she stood wondering which she should take. Then she realized it was right for her to take the staircase. When she and I talked about her dream, she felt that it showed she should be relying on herself and the things she could accomplish, rather than on the mechanical ways of getting well.

A question I hear a lot is, "How do I deal with the stress and terror of having further tests and treatment?"

I suggest that if you are having trouble making a decision about whether to have treatment, you call my voice mail. It has a message that will help you. It will say, "If your problem is marriage, push one. Chemotherapy, two. Radiation, three. Surgery, four. Relationships, five." You push the appropriate button and say, "I don't know if I should have chemotherapy," and the machine says, "Don't have it." And then you say, "But there are things that scare me. The doctor says I could die if I don't have it." The machine says, "Then have it." You say, "But there are lots of side effects." "Oh, then don't have it." About the fourth or fifth time, you laugh and say, "I guess I have to decide." And the machine says, "That's right. You have to make a choice."

A test provides information. You are not giving up your power by having a test; you're gaining knowledge. And if you see it as information, it doesn't become so frightening. I know that at times the information isn't necessarily what you'd like to hear. A cancer can recur, a cardiogram can show heart disease, a blood test can show elevated cholesterol or liver problems. But then the question becomes, "What do I do about this now that I know? Now that I'm empowered, what choices do I have?"

When people ask for advice on how to make a choice I will ask, "If you make such-and-such a choice and your cancer comes back, how will you feel?" And if they say, "Oh, I'll be mad at myself," then I say, "Do everything possible so that you're not mad at yourself. There is no problem being mad at someone else, but you have to live with yourself." It's okay to let your feelings help determine the choice. But if you can't make your own choices, remember to call my voice-mail message.

Your Self-Image During and After Therapy

I remember one lady who said she didn't know whether to have a mastectomy. I asked her to draw a picture of herself with and without a mastectomy, and the results were interesting. In the drawing of herself **with** a mastectomy, she was wearing elaborate makeup and jewelry, as if she had to prove her sexuality and femininity. In the other drawing she was unadorned.

She and I looked at the drawings together, and I shared these insights with her. This helped her open up to her feelings and to make a decision based upon her own needs. When someone feels that surgery is the right choice, then it isn't disfiguring, it's healing. Yes, your body may be different afterward, but there are also some beautiful ways to look at it. One man said to his wife after her breast was removed, "Now my hand can be closer to your heart."

When people do feel disfigured after surgery, they wonder how they can recover their sexuality and feel lovable and beautiful. Part of the process is feeling self-esteem, feeling love toward yourself and allowing yourself to receive affection from those who love you. All of this helps in allowing you to know that you are still lovable.

Cheryl Parsons Darnell (who wrote a poem "The Lessons of Texas") also wrote a poem called "The Geography of My Scars."

She discusses the change in geography of her body altered by a mastectomy and finishes with these lines:

It is not a perfect landscape,
unfit for postcards, calendars or brochures.
But my husband is blind to the surface flaws.
And I see myself through his eyes.
The eyes of a native
who overlooks things
that only a tourist would notice.

You have to think deeply about your identity. Who are you? Are you that missing part of your body? Do you identify with it so closely? I see people who die rather than give up a part of their body. They deny that something is killing them because they're afraid to lose an organ or a limb. I am not judging them, but I feel sorry for them. I don't like to see people make choices out of fear.

I think you are more than your body part. There are many ways to feel sensual, sexual and lovable, and they start from inside you.

I have already mentioned Fay, that special woman from Toronto who was always a fighter. She wrote me to say that once when she was soaking in an herbal bubble bath and listening to one of my tapes, her two young daughters

. . . came quietly into the bathroom and without saying a word, started to wash me as I have so often done with them. They took special care where the mastectomy scar is, then as they washed my other breast, Leslie said, "You know, Mommy, if we are gentle and love your breast, maybe this one won't get sick." Well, of course I started to cry and both girls just hugged me and got soaked and said, "We love you Mommy, so get well in the faraway hospital and bring us a treat." Why does it always take children to teach adults how precious life and love are? Tova still wants to take my prosthesis to school for Show and Tell.

After reading that, I think it's hard to see Fay as anything but whole. There is more to us than our bodies. You can be beautiful in someone else's eyes, even if a part of you is missing.

That certainly is something I've learned about love. The people I love are beautiful. It really doesn't have anything to do with how they look. To me they are beautiful, and that's never going to change.

When Others Are Not Supportive

What happens if you don't have a family that is loving? How do you tell a father or sister or doctor or lover who hasn't been supportive to be supportive? I don't think you can. It would take a very unusual individual to listen to you and then just change. Change is a gradual process.

When you are asking for help from others, always use the word **I**. Speak about **your** needs, about how you feel. Don't tell them what to do or criticize them. Then they can respond without feeling inadequate or judged. They'll be listening, if they're capable, to what you need. I might add that this advice can also apply to those who have no family and must reach out to others.

Make your needs known, and also change the ways you respond to their behavior, so that when they're not supportive you will react in a different way. You can let them know you're not the same old doormat who is going to put up with their unsupportive behavior. When they ask you to continue in old, unhealthy patterns you can say no to something you don't want to do. If you change yourself, you change the people around you.

You can make it clear that others don't have to feel helpless. You are not asking them to cure your problem, but they are capable of helping you and caring for you. You can ask them to listen to you, or to give you a hug, so that they feel empowered in simple ways to help. Part of the reason they may pull away is that they feel helpless. If it is difficult for them, let them know that just as you may say no, they can also. You can let them know what is happening, and what you need, and begin to open up communication.

Most of all, the problem is one of communication. Are you letting people know what you need? If they can't meet your needs because of their inadequacies, then they may never be capable of changing. You may have to accept that. Just get them to do what they can, which might mean some practical ways of helping you, such as driving, calling, or taking you shopping. Or if they are depleting you, get them out of your life. Just as important as getting help is getting those who are draining you out of your life. You don't stop loving them, but they have to be asked to leave.

Unfortunately and sadly, some people are not capable of being the kind of people we need. The best thing you can do is to accept that and not waste energy in conflict but reach out and find others who will give you support.

But if you're determined to change the other people, change yourself and your behavior, and then they'll have to change too.

Sometimes the best response is paradoxical—you can become more like the person who bothers you. If someone tells you you look as though you had only a month to live, tell that person that it's more likely only a week. He or she will have to lighten up and achieve a healthy balance of hope and reality.

What do you do about people who say, "Oh, I'm sure you'll be okay" during treatments? How do you respond? When people tell you you'll be okay, they are really saying they can't tolerate hearing you say anything else. They need to deny, so they are cutting you off. They can't deal with your difficulties. But to keep reassuring them will tire you and may only depress you more. If anybody said to me, "You look great," without asking how I really felt, I'd say, "Oh, no, I feel like I'll be dead next week." Then the person may stop and really begin to listen to me and allow me to talk about my fears and problems. The truth is that when you do share your feelings, you are less likely to have problems with treatment.

I received a letter from a woman who has been dealing with chronic illness for many years. At first her husband was supportive, but recently he has asked for a divorce, as he has found a younger woman he wants to be with. This woman asks how she can rediscover the hope and energy to heal.

My comment is that if you had the courage and energy to do what you did in the past, you will be able to rediscover it. But put the energy into yourself now—the energy that you used to put into the relationship with your husband and in trying to hold on to him. It will mean dealing with all the emotions and the labor pains that will give birth to a new you. Don't hang on to the pain or even to the other person who is draining you. I see in many women a fear of being independent that is even greater than the fear of their disease. I've had people refuse to come to our groups because they were afraid of doing a drawing. One woman had her ten-year-old son do the drawing for her. I know women who have said, "I went home and I changed, but my husband developed chest pains and was hospitalized, so I'm going back to the old ways. It's easier. I'll keep my cancer."

It is sad to hear this from people. Why shouldn't you have the opportunity to live a full life?

Don't be afraid of being on your own. If you can han-

dle the disease, you can handle the loss of your husband.
It may be that you will be better off without this man,
who is not committed to healthy growth and your life. It
may also be that he can't handle the thought of losing
someone he cares for. A new or other woman doesn't
threaten him because he doesn't care for her as deeply.

But change is frightening. Maybe that old "security" isn't there, but I can only emphasize that you are
capable. We are all capable. I'm impressed over and
over again with the women I see who have enormous
fears, yet when I meet them a few years after a traumatic event they're finding themselves—they're happy.
They have confronted their fears; life has become a
challenge. In some cases their children have even said,
"We're worried about Mom, about all the things she's
doing, like white-water rafting and getting into politi-
cal rallies, when she was afraid to go out in the rain or
write a check before."

Discover yourself; give birth to yourself. Let the
old person go and allow yourself to live. Because if
you're living to hang on to somebody else, you're not
living. Fear, not a healthy commitment, is keeping that
relationship going. Devote your life to yourself—not in
a selfish way, but in loving yourself and contributing
love to others. Give yourself to love.

Dealing with Pain

People sometimes talk about trying to "conquer" pain
and about how much energy this takes. But it is important to heal your life and not to try to conquer something, because if you do you'll just wear yourself out.
When a life is healed and free of conflict, pain is man-
ageable. Make the pain your teacher. Learn from it, listen to it.

What is the pain like? What are you experiencing?

Write down the words that fit your pain: squeezing, pressure, knifelike, burning. List all the things in your life that are squeezing you, pressuring you, stabbing you, burning you up. Deal with those issues. This will help heal your life, and the pain will lessen; it will be controllable. Let love into the painful area.

Sometimes it is helpful to see if there is a pattern to the pain. There may be times when it says, "Stop what you're doing"—not that you need pain to give you the freedom to stop. If there are things that you don't want to do, then say no. You don't have to hurt to be free. I sometimes ask people, "What does cancer give you permission to do?" I do this because of a woman who said, "I was angry at you for suggesting that I might get a benefit from my illness. Why did I need an illness? And then I changed your question to 'What did cancer give me permission to do?'" You begin to realize that you don't have to be sick or in pain to have your needs met. You could substitute the word **pain** for **cancer** and ask, "What does the pain give me permission to do?" To not go to work? I see people in pain after surgery, and then when they're declared disabled, the pain goes away. What they really wanted was to stop doing a specific job.

Consider all the things that can help you. Work on finding peace of mind. Then you "conquer" your pain and your fears—not by work that burns up your energy but by an inner peace that heals and restores it.

We're Not Disabled, We're Enabled

A man who was severely injured in an automobile accident came to a workshop and said, "Often what I experience as a disabled person is that people gawk at me, or they turn away. How do I live with this, or how do I change it?"

My answer is that you can't change other people. You can change only yourself. You can begin to see yourself not as disabled but as a person, one who is whole despite the fact that parts of your body may be altered, missing or not functioning. If you change your image of yourself, the way other people deal with you will also be affected. You will be whole.

Some people, however, are always going to be afraid of you—because you represent what could happen to them, and they're afraid they wouldn't be able to handle it. And they may run and never get to know you as a person. That's something you may just have to accept. It isn't you, it's them.

But then there are people who, though they may be frightened, will also watch you. When you are capable of dealing with your disability, you become a teacher and a healer. There are people who have taken away my fears because I realize that I would be capable of doing what they're doing with their afflictions. So the quadriplegic who holds a paintbrush in his mouth, the blind individual who isn't afraid to go to an airport and get on an airplane, or to ski in the Special Olympics—as these people find their way and are not afraid of the world, they take away my fear. They are simply showing us that there are no afflictions that human beings are incapable of dealing with. A blind individual may be more outgoing and assertive with a guide dog than I am with my vision.

Animals can teach us so much. Dr. Donna Lindner, a veterinary surgeon, wrote to me about this, just before she herself was to go into the hospital for a mastectomy. She said:

There is so much that human patients could learn from animal patients. They are so tough that I am

constantly humbled by their courage! I can ampu-
tate a leg or half of a jaw, and within a day or two
they are trying to walk and eat and lick their owners' faces. They seem to have it figured out so
much better than we do. They seem intuitively to
understand that the loss of a body part doesn't
make them any less special to their friends and
family, and that the simple things are what matter
most. All they want is to be warm and fed and
comfortable, to nap in the sun, and to love and be
loved. The only other need I would add, perhaps, is
the need to accomplish what you were put on earth
to accomplish, and actually they probably do that
as well, since it is likely they were put here to love
and be loved, and maybe even to teach us a few
things.

I simply ask people, "Why do you want to live?
How are you managing to continue to love under those
conditions?" One man helped me to understand when
he said, "We're not disabled, we're enabled."

Carol Guion wrote about a young man named John
McGough in the *Noetic Sciences Review* (Autumn,
1992). John was born in 1957 with Down Syndrome.
Everyone discouraged his mother from bringing him
home from the hospital. But she felt that taking care of
him was "what I had to do." John is a remarkable
young man, filled with love for his family members (he
is the second of seven children) and often startling
community members with his sympathy for them at
critical moments.

During a family discussion of the meaning of
"retarded," John gave his definition: "If you cannot
get your love flows going, cannot communicate and
you are not aware who you are, I call that retarded.
Some people are only a little bit retarded. Then I
can help them, because they get curious about me.

They get into communication with me and their love flows get going. Then it works for them if they like. They get more aware."

How do you live with a disability? How do you change it? You change yourself and your attitude toward life. As your image of yourself changes, the image that others have of you—and the relationships you have with them—will change too. You don't try to change other people. Only their difficulties and their pain will transform them. Nothing that you specifically say or do will change them—except perhaps that by living your life and being an example or beacon or torch, you can help light their way.

4
Exploring Inner Space: Body, Mind and Spirit

Images are. . . bridges thrown out towards an unseen shore.

—CARL JUNG
*"ON THE RELATION OF ANALYTICAL
PSYCHOLOGY TO POETRY"*

Symbols do not flow from the unconscious to tell us what we already know, but to show us what we have yet to learn.

—ROBERT A. JOHNSON
"WE"

When the mind is troubled, the body cries out.

—*"GODFATHER III"*

The Fifth Direction:
Into the Darkness

I can't help thinking that if we had taken all the money
we have spent on exploring outer space and used it for
inner-space exploration, on knowing ourselves better,
the world would be a better place, and we would be
happier. I admire our curiosity about the solar system
and what lies around us, but I would also like to know
about our inner systems and what lies within us.

Many of us are frightened to go into our inner
space. Doing so may seem threatening, but I believe
that going into that threat, that fear, is what life is
about. I like to think that there are five directions in
which we can go: east, west, north, south and into our
darkness. That fifth direction can be the source of
great knowledge for us. Healing is a work of darkness.
Think of the five dots on dice. It is the fifth dot, at the
center, that is the key.

I still find it astonishing that as I travel to medical schools and hospitals, almost all doctors tell me that they have never heard that in 1933 Carl Jung listened to a case presentation about a patient's dream and made a correct physical diagnosis of a brain tumor from the dream alone. Why this isn't common knowledge, why it isn't taught, I have no idea, because dreams are incredibly powerful and informative. They can aid in making physical diagnoses, just as drawings can, and they can change people's lives. For me as a physician it is a routine question to ask people "What are your dreams? What are your images?" and to have them draw symbols to help guide them.

If we were open to this kind of information, and if physicians were open to it, we would see more diagnoses of this kind. As a doctor I have no hesitancy in using dreams and drawings as a part of my work, to make physical diagnoses and to help decide on a type of therapy. It doesn't mean that I don't do all the other things I was trained to do as a physician, but this is an important part of the process for me.

Why is it so hard for the medical profession to accept the idea that the mind influences the body, or that the two constitute a unit? Perhaps because we're simply not taught in medical school that you can't separate your thoughts and your mind from your body. But the fact is that our thoughts and beliefs affect us physically as well as psychologically, and people can change. Recent studies have shown that even genes are capable of change.

Therapists sometimes write to me about their research for Ph.D. and master's work; it shows the beneficial effects of imagery and relaxation techniques on both the physical aspects of a disease and the psychological and mental aspects. And this includes children and families. We are now seeing benefits with cancer, AIDS, infertility, miscarriages and many more disease states. The American Cancer Society is now training physicians and nurses in psycho–social care techniques.

Recently I had a dream in which I walked into my former surgical practice. I was naked, and everyone looked at me. I said, "What's the matter, haven't you ever seen a naked doctor before?" I was totally at peace and comfortable. The staff came running out trying to find a white jacket for me to wear, but they couldn't find one. I woke up thinking about that dream. To me it meant that I was revealing myself, letting people know the real me. I wasn't afraid to appear naked, and I felt totally comfortable; they were the ones who were uncomfortable. They couldn't find anything to fit me, perhaps because in a sense I don't fit in. I like to think I am being different and unique. If you put together the words "**C**razy, **U**nique, **R**efreshing and **E**xceptional," they spell CURE.

We are told in the Bible that God speaks to us in dreams and visions. I believe we ought to look at our dreams and symbols and see what they can tell us about our deeper awareness and knowledge, both on a psychological and physical level, so that we can get in touch with this primal, creative, intelligent energy.

Some religions warn us that the Devil may appear if we close our eyes and create images. I am more concerned about some of us never meeting God. I think we can recognize the Devil if he shows up.

Images and Dreams Can Help Heal the Body

Whether we are asking "Who should I marry?" "What profession should I follow?" or "What is happening in my body?" answers are available to us from the unconscious if we can interpret our images.

Some symbols are collective, or universal—we all share them, and we are made aware of them by the common themes in myths. Other symbols are individual, and you must determine their meaning as it relates to your life.

To try to interpret your own symbols by yourself may be difficult. It is easier to work with someone who has training, so that that person can act as a guide— particularly a Jungian therapist or someone trained in imagery. You can read about dream work, myths and fairy tales, and you can keep a record of your dreams and symbols and begin to discern frequent images and patterns. You are the expert on your own symbols. Let them guide you.

When it comes to choices about therapy, images can help us. A woman who had a radical mastectomy for cancer of the breast as well as a liver biopsy learned that she had metastatic cancer to her liver and that there were many spots throughout the liver. One of the nurses gave her my books and tapes. She wrote me to say that one day she was resting on the sofa, consciously having nothing on her mind, when she saw:

> . . . a group of crusaders in armor, on white horses, cascading down a hill, fighting dirty, filthy beings and being victorious. . . It dawned on me that my body was trying to tell me I needed to do imaging. I remember your saying that one of your patients had used scrubbly bubbles. . . I started visualizing scrubbly bubbles but I armed them with vacuum cleaners, scrub brushes, pails, mops and brooms. I added a few hammers and chisels for those stubborn cancer cells and so the vacuum cleaners came right behind.

Some time later, when she was admitted to the hospital with a high fever and a very low white count, her images spontaneously changed. She could only see a tall pipe with bubbles coming out of it. Her surgeon told her that her count had jumped to 5000.

> He said the white cells were manufactured in the bone. I cut off listening and exclaimed, "The bone, as in a pipe or tube!" It was suddenly so clear. My body was telling me the white cells were producing like crazy and that was why the bubbles were spilling out of the tube.

She went home, continued her imaging, and several weeks later went to see her oncologist:

> As he was reading my latest CAT scan I saw an involuntary head motion toward my chart, as if he was surprised at what he was reading. I prayed a silent prayer. He then turned to me and said, "Your liver is clear." I praised God and jumped up and almost knocked the dear sweet man over trying to hug him. I told him I thought it was a miracle, due to two things, prayer and maybe the chemo.

A woman named Ruth Richman wrote to me about having severe pain in her lower abdomen. She was being treated by various doctors with pain killers and hormones. She wrote:

> I realized that my body knew what was going on and that what was best for me was to listen to my body. After two or three months of talking to myself and making my mind receptive to messages, I had a dream. I awoke four times during the night, but each time I fell back asleep into the same dream. In my dream was a very gentle nonthreatening man carrying a knife. The knife scared me, but not the man. The knife was not bloody. The dream was not gory. The man never attacked me. He was just there with the knife. Everywhere I went he

would appear carrying the knife. When I awoke for the final time, I sat up and thought about this odd dream and then it hit me. I knew with certainty that I was going to need surgery but that it was going to be okay and that the surgery was the right thing to do.

During all this time I was also praying that God would direct my actions. I asked for a consultation with my ob-gyn doctor. Rationally and openly I told him I wanted him to remove my left ovary. We discussed all of my options and then we agreed on surgery. I went into it with the assurance that I was doing the right thing. I had my left tube and ovary and uterus removed. After the pathology report came back we found I had a fast-growing benign tumor inside my uterus on the left side.

She recalled telling a friend before the surgery about her dream, about how the man was "nonthreatening, just a benign sort of person." She said,

I never realized the significance of this until the pathology report came back. My body knew all along and all I needed to do was listen.

Mary Deane-Scalora said that when she developed myasthenia gravis, her doctor told her that as therapy she should have her thymus removed. But she said, "The thymus is the kindergarten for my immune system. I don't think I want it removed right now." As her disease progressed she became weaker and weaker. Finally she and her husband discussed possible courses of treatment and hoped that her unconscious might give her some guidance through a dream.

She said, "That night I had a dream. I saw my thymus, and it was gray, with fingerlike extensions into me. I asked my doctor the next day, without telling him what had happened, 'What does a normal thymus look like?' He described it, and I said, 'Oh, then mine isn't normal. Take it out.'" After her thymectomy, when the tubes were removed and she was again able to speak, she asked her surgeon, "What did my thymus look like?" He held his hand up, curled the fingers and said, "Well, it was gray with fingerlike extensions." What this dream did, of course, was to help her choose surgery, and to let her know this was the right therapy for her, not an assault or mutilation. Her thymus contained a malignant thymoma.

Drawings Are Messages, Too

Just as your dreams are messages from inside you, so are your drawings, and these can also be used in healing. I know I can go anywhere in the world with a box of crayons and communicate with people, because we are of common origin. But it is important to realize that the images must be your own. The woman I mentioned dreamed of knights, but for someone else that could create conflict.

A Quaker will have trouble killing a cancer and will need to heal through nonviolence and love.

A friend had suggested to a woman with a large chest tumor that she use the symbol of dogs to represent her white blood cells, but she felt uncomfortable with that image. Instead she saw the tumor as a block of ice, and her therapy and spirituality as warm sunshine entering her body. The tumor essentially melted away.

Children, too, have their own images. Some don't mind fighting wars against their disease—they'll draw pictures of dragons gobbling up their cancer cells, or armies blasting those cells. Or they'll put their disease in a frying pan and sizzle it. We have to allow each person to express himself or herself in their own unique way.

As a guide I can constructively criticize. One problem I have run into is that people may talk about the picture they want to do in one way but draw it in another. I remember a man who described hundreds of thousands of white cells and only a hundred cancer cells; but he actually drew the picture with many cancer cells and only one white cell. So it is important that the drawing really be looked at.

Sometimes I use drawings to help families understand concepts. When people feel that they are not getting enough support from their families, or that their treatments are poisonous or destructive, you can get into intellectual arguments. But when the family sees the symbols drawn by the person—being alone, isolated, or being a skeleton in a coffin—then we can really communicate and deal with the situation.

Two books are available that can help you interpret drawings: Susan Bach's *Life Paints Its Own Span* and *The Secret World of Drawings* by Gregg Furth.

Susan Bach, a Jungian therapist in London, has worked with children who are confronting serious illness, and she has them do spontaneous drawings. She looks at the drawings with the children and asks them to discuss their pictures. She has seen in the drawings, as I have, that children often know when disease is present, whether treatment will work, whether they are going to survive—all of these things are there on the paper. Sometimes we can see these things from the children's symbols even without the children or adults being there to interpret.

Bach's and Furth's work will help you understand the significance of using certain colors in drawings and of the placement of objects on the page. You can also gain insight if you simply save your drawings, date them, and then look at them again in a few weeks or months. Sometimes there is a configuration, a color, a symbol, an evolution of objects that will leap out at you later when you may not even have noticed it at

first. Even with all my experience in this area, I learn
from my drawings—the unconscious takes over and
you are blinded to things that you have put on the
paper until you go back later and intellectually look at
it. The same is true of what you see or don't see on a
printed page.

As we change internally, our drawings also change.
Dr. Rachel Naomi Remen, a wonderful physician,
wrote an article called "Spirit: Resource for Healing,"
in the Autumn 1988 issue of *Noetic Sciences Review.*
She describes a patient who had cancer of the leg; the
leg was amputated in order to save his life. He was
twenty-four years old, very angry and bitter. He felt a
deep sense of injustice and a hatred for healthy people.
Dr. Remen says:

> After working with this man for a couple of years I
> saw a profound shift. He began "coming out of
> himself." He began visiting other people in the hos-
> pital who had suffered severe physical losses and
> he would tell me the most wonderful stories about
> these visits. Once he visited a young woman who
> was almost his own age. It was a hot day and he
> was in running shorts so his artificial leg showed
> when he came into her hospital room. The woman
> was so depressed about the loss of both her breasts
> that she wouldn't even look at him, wouldn't pay
> attention to him. The nurses had left her radio
> playing, probably in order to cheer her up. So, des-
> perate to get her attention, he unstrapped his leg,
> dropped it to the floor with a "bang" and began
> dancing around the room on one leg, snapping his
> fingers to the music. She looked at him in amaze-
> ment, and then she burst out laughing and said,
> "Man, if you can dance, I can sing."
>   At the end of a person's therapy, you do a
> review and the patient talks about what was signifi-
> cant and you share what was significant to you as a

therapist working with that person. He and I were reviewing our two years of work when I opened his file and found several drawings he had made. I wanted to return them to him. "Oh, look at this," I said. At the beginning of our work together, I had suggested to him that he draw a picture of his body. And he had taken a black crayon and drawn a picture of a vase. Running through the vase he drew a deep crack. With his black crayon he had drawn the crack over, and over, and over. He was grinding his teeth with rage at the time. It was very painful, because it seemed to me that this vase could never function as a vase again. It could never hold water. This was his image of his body.

Now, two years later, I returned this picture to him. He looked at it and said, "Oh, this one isn't finished." And I said, extending the box of crayons, "Why don't you finish it." Smiling, he picked a yellow crayon and putting his finger on the crack he said, "You see here, this is where the light comes through." And with the yellow crayon he drew light streaming through the crack in his body.

All of us could gain by using these techniques. They are empowering, and they lead to transformation because they come from within. I always feel that when you look at your own drawing and discover something, it's like a light bulb coming on. People say, "Wow, that's my truth, my message." It is far more easily accepted than words from an outside authority.

Your Emotions Are Chemical

Laughter and joy can mean a healing, life-enhancing message going to every cell in your body, whereas

shame, guilt and despair can lead to destructive messages. Your emotions are chemical. It is exciting to
understand that specific thoughts can create changes in
the body. When you are happy, your body knows it.
When you're depressed and feeling hopeless, your
body also knows that. And when I refer to your body I
mean your bone marrow, the lining of your blood ves-
sels, your liver. Every organ participates in the happiness or the sadness. Consciousness and knowledge
occur at the cell membrane. (Candace Pert, a neuro-
physiologist, has done work with neuropeptides and in
essence feels that awareness and consciousness will
ultimately be located at the cell membrane.)

We know that the happy individual has a different
set of neuropeptides (hormones) circulating from those
of the person who is depressed, angry or anxious. Our
nervous system and other organ systems through these
neuropeptides are communicating with every cell in
our bodies. Our gut feelings, how we deal with life,
how many white cells we produce, how rapidly a
wound heals—all of these are linked.

Francis Hodgson Burnett describes this well in *The
Secret Garden*, a favorite book of my wife's from her
elementary-school years (which I recently read also):

> One of the new things people began to find out in
> the last century was that thoughts—just mere
> thoughts—are as powerful as electric batteries—as
> good for one as sunlight is, or as bad for one as
> poison. To let a sad thought or a bad one get into
> your mind is as dangerous as letting a scarlet fever
> germ get into your body. If you let it stay there after
> it has got in you may never get over it as long as
> you live.

If you visualize a change happening in your body
(you don't have to know anatomy to create a satisfac-
tory image), the body will respond. If you picture more

blood going to your wounded leg, then indeed more blood will flow there. The mind and body are not two separate entities, they are one; we are a unit.

In addition to our emotions, the mind and body also communicate through visualization and meditation. These can provide another doorway to the unconscious, to our true path and healing.

What Happens During Meditation

I think it is important to interrupt your day every few hours for meditation, prayer or imagery—a healing interval. I don't care what you name it. I am not asking you to do something you can fail at or something you don't want to do. You can be guided by an audio tape, or you can simply listen to music, look at flowers, say a prayer. But do give yourself some time every few hours to be open to that inner knowledge and healing.

At a workshop one day we were doing a meditation exercise, and afterward a woman said she had been afraid. She said, "While I was meditating and 'took a trip inside myself' as you suggested, I felt threatened and tearful. Why?"

I think that many of us are very good at keeping a lid on ourselves; we don't deal with our feelings. When we start to meditate and to relax our conscious control, it is as though we are taking the lid off. Things stored inside us begin to come out.

When this happens people become emotional. They may cry. It isn't necessarily that tragic or fearful events come up but that meditating is a release, and we want to stay "in control."

The idea that we are in control at all is an illusion, because at a deep level, in our unconscious minds, we are still suffering things we've repressed. Most of us are afraid to pay attention to and to use this wonderful tool of the unconscious, which is there to help and guide us.

Bobbie began to notice that numbers played a key role in many of the drawings that people did in our workshops. The number of trees in a picture, the numbers on which the hands of a clock were set, the quantity of rays of the sun—counting these has helped people discover things that have been stored inside them. Carl Jung said, "In this connection, I always come upon the enigma of the natural number. I have a distinct feeling that number is a key to the mystery that is just as much discovered as it is invented. It is quantity as well as meaning." An excellent book on this subject is *Number and Time* by Marie-Louise von Franz (Northwestern Press, 1974).

If you are with a group of people who are being guided in an imagery session, remember you are free **not** to follow the leader's directions if something is traumatic or difficult and you are not ready to deal with it.

If a meditation refers to lying on the beach and enjoying the surf or the sunshine and you had a family member drown at the ocean, the meditation is not going to be very pleasant for you. A meditation should be suited to you.

You can stop. You don't have to follow a leader. You can open your eyes. You can visualize something else. You're in charge of the images.

What if you are not visual? A woman asked, "What do you do with people who have trouble visualizing? I think in conversations, study languages, process everything verbally. Music is nice but I don't find it therapeutic. Is there a way to use language to visualize?"

Playwrights do this. Arthur Miller, in an interview, said that while he is working on a play he hears the characters speaking inside his head, and he writes down what they are saying. If you are verbal you can select a prayer, a mantra, and repeat it to yourself. Doing so may help relax you.

You can talk to yourself, talk to your body. People may say to their heart, "Slow down." They may tell themselves that they are on a swing, which suggests a steady rhythm, and then the heart can go back to that rhythm. They aren't necessarily creating a picture; they are describing a process, and for verbal people that can be effective.

Some of us have a strong visual sense, some are primarily auditory, others are olfactory or tactile. We have to make use of our individual senses. Don't set yourself up to be a failure by trying to use senses or techniques that are not appropriate for you. Listen to your own speech. Do you talk about "seeing," or "getting in touch with," or "listening to"? Understanding your speech will help you find your sensory type.

If you are interested in visualizing and have difficulty doing it, working with an art therapist or hypnotherapist can help open up those areas. You are capable of using these techniques, and they can be tailored to you.

I know people who have used the piano as part of their visualization; they have literally made piano playing their imagery, as Fay did. It is the peace and the beauty that come with the playing that provide the healing. Someone who is a drummer may be healed by music, an artist may be healed by what she sees, another individual by a change in feelings.

Just being still can also be a meditation. This is something I learned many years ago when I injured my back. I was impatient to do things, but I gradually realized that I had to learn to be still to heal, and I had to see being still as doing something.

For some of us this can be the hardest thing we have ever learned. We feel that the only value in our lives is related to what we do, not to who we are or are being. But by being yourself you are doing something important. Being still and caring for yourself is an activity. Sometimes the most valuable thing you can do is simply wait, rest, be motionless, and let yourself heal. (If you find this hard to do, I can write you a prescription.)

The beauty of stillness makes me think of these lines from the Bible:

> And behold, the Lord passed by, and a great and
> strong wind rent the mountains, and brake in
> pieces the rocks before the Lord; but the Lord was
> not in the wind. And after the wind an earthquake;
> but the Lord was not in the earthquake. And after
> the earthquake a fire; but the Lord was not in the
> fire. And after the fire a still small voice.
> —*I Kings 19:11–12*

Please, listen to that voice.

The Power of Symbols

One gentleman wrote to me about an experience he had had in the hospital. The predictions were that he had about six months to live and that he should think about getting his affairs in order. This stripped away all of his hope. His doctor's prognosis was given in a small underground chamber, after which he was transported back to his hospital room through a long corridor: "That ride became the visual and physical metaphor for my full recovery."

He said that the first half of the passageway leading from the tumor institute to the hospital declined to a point midway, then turned to a slight incline as one approached the hospital:

As I rode away from the institute on the down slope, there could not have been a lower emotional state. My life seemed to be caving in around me, yet just as we reached the lowest point of the passageway, I glanced ahead and realized that I was facing an upward climb. It was a small thing at the time, but it was the spark of hope and inspiration I needed. The uphill choice was mine and I chose to live. From then on, despite a second operation and six weeks of radiation, I knew in my heart I would return to full health.

He is well 20 years later.

What is significant is what he "knew in my heart." It all starts with a belief—down to every cell in your body. You must believe to have it happen.

This man has since become an instructor of transcendental meditation courses and techniques, and he talks about helping start a course in communication for physicians. He doesn't feel that they are different in a sense from lawyers, accountants or engineers—that all of us are trained in the physical aspects of our jobs and the information we need to have, but not in how to communicate it to people. I certainly agree with him and with the fact that our words and symbols can heal us. (As I will discuss later, the opposite is also true—we can destroy people with our words and symbols.)

A woman named Isaacsen-Bright described how she dreamed of a grotto, with stones and ferns surrounding a lovely pool. She jumped into the water; it was warm and wonderful, bubbly, clear.

I opened up the soles of my feet and let everything drain out that wasn't of any use to me anymore, that I needed to slough off. And I dove and paddled. As I looked up there was a sign and it read, "I am well." I was delighted. How kind of them to do this for me. I dove down again and came up. And the sign said, "I AM WELL." I knew I had found my core, my source, my I AM. And I dove deeper and cleansed myself. I felt so rich. When I came up I glanced to my left and far away I could see all the choices that had started at the beginning of time and had culminated in me. I saw the holiness of me in each and every one of us and how we, each one, are the sum of so many choices too.

It is wonderful when the inner voice does let us know, through these images, that we are lovable and beautiful. And that we can accept this at a deep level of our being.

Judy Hogan wrote to me about a symbol that had special meaning to her:

The first sign I received that told me I was on the right path, and that it would be a grand one regard-less of the outcome, was an artichoke from my gar-den. My husband and I have a small garden of strawberries and artichokes, parsley, rhubarb, pota-toes and salad vegetables. A winter freeze had killed our very successful artichokes and for two years we had failed with our new plants. However, that year, amidst our very busy family, work and civic schedules, we had succeeded in growing strong plants, and one had a blossom. I vowed to let this blossom mature and bloom out as I had with our successful plants.

One day in late September I realized that the plant with the blossom was dying. I felt guilty for not paying more attention to this problem, for clearly we would lose the plant. However, the week-end I spotted it was just after school had begun and I had planned to can fruits and vegetables in my "extra" time. I didn't have time to do this even, for I was exhausted by the onslaught of the school year's beginning. (I taught at two schools and the schedule was ridiculously demanding.)

So, in a quick fix, I hacked off the artichoke and threw it in the trash, with great sadness—not about the loss of the plant, but rather that my life had become so scheduled and hurried that I had no time for the me that would in prior years have saved the artichoke and found some arrangement in the house for it. I stood at the trash can for ten minutes or more with the painful revelation that that part of me, which I considered to be the best because it took in life and nature and recognized the spirituality of the larger picture of the world and my place in it, was almost dead. I had pushed it away so long that on this day I could barely get a quiver from it deep inside me. I realized I would never be me again if my present trend continued. Though my time of putting art and my other nature aside because of children and family and outside responsibilities was coming to an end because my youngest child would be in college the following year, I knew then and there, holding the dead artichoke, that I wasn't going to make it—the damage was practically irreparable.

In a fit of anger, panic and hope, I retrieved the artichoke, vowing to take it to the high school to my friend who teaches watercolors, hoping she could use it for a still life. It was a small gesture, but it was a beginning, a desperate cry out to myself to save that part of me I had willed away—my very being.

On Monday I took the artichoke to school and left it on my friend's desk. I was happy she could use it and that it had a home. Its tightly closed petals, unique shape and color would provide a challenge to the students and a point of texture and interest to their paintings.

That Wednesday, Judy and her friend went off
to an art conference in Portland, where Judy also
saw her doctor. The next day she learned she had
ovarian cancer and had surgery. After getting her
to the hospital, her friend stayed with her until her
husband arrived. When her friend returned to
school, there sitting on her desk was the artichoke, in full gorgeous bloom. Later that week
her husband brought it back to her in her hospital
room, in a tuna fish can that had been painted by
the art teacher. When Judy Hogan saw that artichoke, she said, "it was an indication that, though
things looked bleak, there was always hope. There
was time for me to bloom, even though recent
developments pointed to the lopped-off part of
my spirit lying in the bottom of the trash can."

That's what I feel—that if you can just go on being
an artichoke, you don't question your statistics or your
odds. I think that's part of the reason this lady is alive
today. That artichoke showed her what the spirit and
nature can do.

In his book *Inner Work,* Robert A. Johnson states
that Carl Jung:

believed that God needs human agencies to assist
in the incarnation of his creation. As Thomas Mann
observed in *Joseph and His Brothers,* "God needed
the ladder in Jacob's dream as a way to come and
go between heaven and earth." The visions of
human beings make such a ladder and transmit
information into the collective conscious of humanity. No "practicality" beyond this is required.

Keep reaching for your personal goal. It may seem
beyond your grasp, but one day a ladder may appear,
and you can climb up to attain it.

For me, there is a complete circle. We are all part of the same system. The mind, body and spirit are all integrated, and in our imagery we can find the presence of love and spirituality. We can allow ourselves to be empowered, to induce self-healing through the creative aspects of poetry, music, art and images and let them work within us to help cure our disease and heal our lives.

5
Helping Others: There Is Always a Way

I have heard of the rainbows, of the stars, of the play of light upon the waves. These I would like to see. But far more than sight, I wish for my ears to be opened. The voice of a friend, the happy busy noises of community, the imaginations of Mozart. . . . Life without these is darker by far than blindness.

—HELEN KELLER

Listening Heals

When our children were growing up, if they came to me with their troubles I usually suggested solutions for them—join a group, see a therapist, take vitamins. They said, "You're no help." But when I sat and listened, they thanked me for what I did and told me how much I had helped them.

I saw this with our therapy groups, too. I would sometimes sit there stunned, my mouth open, not saying anything. As the months went by, people began thanking me for what I had done. What had I done? I hadn't given them any magical cures or answers; I had just listened.

When someone you love has difficulties, listen. When you're feeling terrible that you can't provide a cure, listen. When you don't know what to offer the people you care about, listen, listen, listen.

I sometimes ask people in workshops whether they would rather be blind or deaf. I ask you now to close your eyes and imagine what your world would be like if you could not see, ever again. And then after a few minutes, go turn on the television set; turn the sound off and just watch the picture. Think about how your life would be if you could not hear. It's not that a person's choice is right or wrong, not that it is better or worse to be blind or deaf; we each might have our preferences. But in my mind blindness separates us from objects, whereas deafness separates us from people.

At the opening of this chapter I quote the words of Helen Keller, blind and deaf from the age of nineteen months. She speaks most eloquently about the healing power of listening when she says, ". . . far more than sight, I wish for my ears to be opened." I know deaf people can learn to listen with their hearts, but please be aware of the power of listening.

Sometimes I think about starting a company called "Therapeutic Airlines," because if you get on an airplane, turn to the person next to you, and say, "I'm a psychologist, what do you do?" for the next several hours you will be told all that person's troubles. Your seatmate will just pour it all out. And then he or she will thank you when the trip is over. So Therapeutic Airlines would be an airline that takes off from a local airport and goes up in the air for two hours. The plane will be full of strangers, we'll tell each other all about our lives, and then we'll come back to where we started and will all feel better.

Don't ever forget the power of listening and the strength it takes just to be there—not curing, but caring. The world is in need of listeners. Picture a child lying in a mother's arms. As Ashley Montagu says, the world needs to be like a loving mother.

When a Child Is Sick: Empowering a Child

Think for a moment about Helen Keller's parents. How did they respond to a nineteen-month-old child who suddenly became blind and deaf? That is something all parents have to consider. What are you willing to accept, and what are you willing to work for? If your child has cancer, AIDS, a brain injury, a congenital disease, are you willing to work at it and not accept a verdict and a sentence? That is important. Because if you are going to feel like a failure, or as if you have done something wrong if you don't achieve a cure, then perhaps it's better not to try. I know that with one of our children I would not accept that philosophy; I would reach out to achieve whatever I could.

A mother wrote me to ask, "How can I make your ideas fit a four-year-old? How can I take what you are teaching and scale it down? You are emphasizing getting control of your life, but how can a child get control? How do I make my daughter's attitude toward herself as positive as possible? And how does one know if a four-year-old is at peace with herself and her surroundings? Doesn't a four-year-old feel powerless?"

First of all, let me say that children have been my greatest teachers. I originally specialized in pediatric surgery, and the children helped me learn by being open, honest and truthful. I was then capable of caring for adults in the same way. So let the honesty and the openness of the child in yourself guide you.

This mother asks many good questions, and some of my answers come from other parents, who have discovered ways. But she can also look at what she is asking and not be overwhelmed. How do you do that? By looking at what brings joy to the child. Take one item at a time, to empower your child in simple ways. Don't look at "control," look at peace of mind. Look at the support that you can give. There are many things we can't control but that we can get through and deal with.

In the doctor's office, if the doctor wants the child on the examining table he or she may say, "Well, let's have you up on the table," and the child can say, "No." But if the doctor says, "Shall I lift you up, or do you want to climb up?" the child has been given some power. Children who are wise and resistant will just give the doctor a smart look and say to themselves, "Okay, he's a wiseguy. I won't answer that one. He's got me." But others will say, "All right, I'll climb up by myself." They can show you how capable they are. In the hospital the doctor may ask, "Which vein would you like the IV in?" Then the child is being empowered.

What some families have done is to hang a large posterboard on the wall of their child's hospital room. Everyone who is going to examine the child must draw a picture. One family had everyone make a handprint and sign it. What this does, obviously, is empower the child. Because if someone comes in, including the professor of pediatrics, and says, "I want to examine you" or "I want to draw some blood," the child can say, "No, not unless you draw a picture or do a handprint and sign it." It is wonderful to watch the professor become insecure and say, "Well, I'm not an artist," and the child answers, "Then you can't examine me." The child becomes the one in charge. Believe me, the child always wins and can go home with a board full of wonderful drawings by all the people who cared for him or her, and it can be framed and hung on the wall.

Your child might also do what one woman did— she insisted that people pay her by giving hugs or by rubbing her bald head if they wanted to "poke or prod or listen to or feel my lymph nodes or my lungs or heart murmur or fiddle with my IV." A child can do the same thing. A hug, a pat on the head—there are many ways that people can pay and show their affection.

Play games with your child. Write a song or a poem; paint a picture. Bring humor in. Let her be childlike, and learn and listen to her. She will let you know how she feels. Don't be afraid to use words like **cancer**. Don't tell people not to talk, because then your child will stop talking, to protect you.

Let her be creative, too, and write a book for other children with cancer. I remember when several nurses came to me to say they had six teenagers who were very ill, and they didn't know how to support them, or what to do. I said, "Get those teenagers and their families to write a book for other teenagers and families." Six months later I received a wonderful book that is an inspiration for everyone and that I'm sure helped heal those families.

Use drawings to discover how your child feels about the treatment. A family came to my office— mother, father and teenage daughter—with a drawing the girl had made of her therapy. The parents said she would no longer go to the hospital for treatment. The picture showed the girl holding a spear and saying, "I hate you." The words **bald**, **ugly** and **horrible** were printed on the drawing, with arrows pointing at her. In the corner of the picture was a cancer cell crying and saying, "Help me." When I asked the girl, "Who do you hate?" she said, "Oh, I hate the doctors. They made me bald, ugly and horrible." She had more sympathy for the cancer, and she wanted to put the spear in her doctor. This was a struggle for the parents. How do you get your child, who hates the doctor, to go back for treatment? This is what can happen if we don't allow the child to participate.

It may mean simple things like having treatment on Monday so that she can be with friends on the weekend, rather than have treatment on Friday and have her feel sick all weekend. It may mean organizing a program at school for teachers and students, to help them understand and support students with cancer.

Remember that children are very suggestible; you can use suggestions in a therapeutic way. You might have "appetite pills" for your child, or "hair-growing salve." These things can change her attitude. Let her talk to other children at school who have had cancer. I'm sure your child isn't the only one. They will support each other. It is wonderful when you talk to children who have had cancer, and if you ask them what they would do for another child in the school, they will tell you how well they would defend that child. So bring the children together—they will help heal one another.

Join organizations like "Candlelighters" so that you can hear from other families, and again, bring siblings and children together for support. Let the doctor know what you are doing. If you show up with your child one day and the doctor says, "Your white count is down today, no chemotherapy," the child may say, "Oh, I'm going to die, I'm not getting treatment." But you can remind her that there are other resources, and you can talk about "your nutrition, your vitamins, your visualization—they're keeping you strong too."

How do you know if a four-year-old is at peace? I'd say, ask her about her feelings and dreams, and look at her drawings. If your home is filled with love, if her parents are loving, then the child will be at peace. So ask yourself the question: "Am I at peace?" If your child has love, she will find peace.

As noted earlier, Jason Gaes wrote a beautiful book called *My Book for Kids with Cansur*, which has helped children as well as adults. I often quote from his book at workshops. He turned his disease into a gift. He writes (the spellings are his):

If you can find it, get a poster that says, "Help me to remember, Lord, that nothing is going to happen today that You and me can't handle together." Then hang it in your room and read it at night when you're scared. If you get scared and can't quit, go and talk to your mom and she can rock you or rub your hair. . .

"Sometimes when you're sick from a treetment you miss school, but try to make your work because collij makes you have all your work done before you can be a doctor. And I'm going to be a doctor who takes care of kids with cansur so I can tell them what it's like.

In one page Jason tells what it takes me an entire book to say, because he is a native. He has also been one of my teachers—though I spell better than he does.

Another young man who has moved me very much is Michael Lidington. After a doctor told Michael that there was nothing more that she could do for him, and left the room in tears, Michael said to his mother, "I never want to be a doctor."

"Why not, Michael?" his mother asked.

"Because I never want to have to tell that to a child."

After his cancer went into remission, he wrote a poem called "I Won!!!":

The cancer's gone, I'm free once more;
I've decided not to walk through the door.
I'll leave this place when the time is right;
Be it during the day or late at night,
But if I'm not ready, then count on a fight!

My family and friends have helped me through;
A lot of the time, not knowing what to do.
If they only knew I'd do the same for them;
They'd understand they're MY life's precious gems

No one will ever quite understand,
The pain which feeds the pen in my hand.
I know they would,
They wish they could,
But until they do I'm alone in this land.

It's time for my life to get a move on;
To break away from the plague I've carried so long.
It's time for me to live again;
To pull my life around this bend.

Thank you those who worried so;
But I'm not going to die, (I told you so!).

To those who need it, take my hand;
I'll guide you through this savage land.

I told Michael that I liked his poem, but not its title, because he was a winner by his fight and attitude whether his cancer came back or not.

His cancer did come back, but a poem that he wrote to be read by his brother at his funeral contained the message that I had wanted him to understand (see p. 217).

I believe that love banishes all disease, and the absence of love is the only true disease. If you cannot understand this, talk to someone who has an illness without love and to someone who has it with love. I'm not saying this to create guilt, or to make you feel "I didn't love enough," but so that we can understand what true healing is about. Hopefulness, the feeling of control, the security of the parents—all of these comfort the child. If a child is loved, he or she is safe, for nothing can happen to be afraid of. And that includes disease and death. As one child said, "My mother was there when I was born, and she'll be there when I die." Just picture a child with a life-threatening illness lying in a crib in the hospital, with his parents lying next to him. Is that child all right? Is that child healed? Will that child be able to deal with whatever comes? My answer is yes, because of the love that envelops that child and that family.

When you are there, your child can face difficulties and transitions surrounded by love.

How can you and your partner continue lovemaking while he or she is ill?

First of all, you have to look at the question: What is lovemaking? I'll never forget the woman with the distended abdomen who said, "My husband and I hug by getting our shoulders and knees around my stomach." That was lovemaking.

So, lovemaking is contact, it is touch. Remember that our physiology is changed by touch. Newborns gain more weight than babies fed the same amount who aren't touched. Touching lets them know they are loved and changes their chemistry. Understand that touching your loved one will change him or her also, and affect the body. Adolescents on a psychiatric ward who were massaged had less anxiety than those who were not massaged. Even the staff became jealous.

Your neuropeptides are altered by touch. I often interrupt my evening lectures—which go on for a couple of hours—by having people stand, turn, and massage the neck and shoulders of the person next to them; then they turn, and the favor is repaid. There is often spontaneous applause after this is done, and I ask people, "Why are you applauding?" Well, they are applauding the way they feel because they've been touched. The sad part is that the role of touch is so little understood. But the University of Miami has opened an Institute of Touch, and gradually we are making therapeutic massage a recognized health-care profession. The majority of states don't recognize it as such, however, and I think it is vitally important that we do recognize that touch plays an enormous role in our interactions and healing.

Regarding sexual activity, I ask you first of all how you feel about yourself and your body. I'd let you know that you are not rejected. A breast may be missing, there may be a colostomy, prostate surgery, difficulties having an erection, or a dry vagina. If you're feeling ugly, unlovable, or incapable of functioning, all of these things are going to affect your desire to participate in lovemaking.

If your partner does not feel like making love, try not to feel rebuffed or rejected. Let him or her know your needs too. Touch the person—your lover, your spouse. Let them know you can touch their body and accept them, and how much their touch means to you. Let them know that they are not their disease. As one woman said, "I'm not the ugliness of my disease." Know that there is beauty in the person and then touch and let the love come. Different positions can help; so can asking the individual what he or she would like. Ask how you can participate, how you can help, so that they feel comfortable with their body, knowing that they are not really very different, whether there is a disease or not. Demonstrate your love and caring. When a husband who has a full head of hair and a beard goes into the bathroom, shaves off his hair and beard, comes out, looks at his wife who's lost her hair because of chemotherapy, and says, "Now what?" she bursts into laughter and is healed by his act.

If you do these things, then even though sexual intercourse may be difficult or impossible, lovemaking is always possible. At times when the organs involved in sexual activity are missing, we can still satisfy our partner by performing for them even when we ourselves cannot participate fully. That's really giving love and pleasure out of love to someone else. And it comes when a relationship has reached a very deep level of commitment.

The Primary Caregiver

Sometimes the caregiver is more motivated than the patient. When the cancer patient cannot, because of mental or physical incapacity, be the exceptional patient, then must the primary caregiver become an exceptional caregiver?

I don't think the issue is whether one is exceptional or not. It is inappropriate to ask more of the caregiver because the patient is not capable of doing certain things. I think the caregiver's role is the same, no matter what the patient is like. That role is to let the patients have their disease, to supply them with material and information that will allow them to make choices and to be exceptional if they choose to be. It's also to not make them or oneself feel like a failure. The caregiver must let the patients have their disease—it is not the caregiver's.

In my book *Peace, Love & Healing*, I list ways in which you, the primary caregiver, can care for yourself so that you don't get sick because you're taking care of another person. You too need your support people, your therapy. It means reaching out, and if you considered that exceptional, I'd say "Yes." But I'd also say that that is normal, healthy behavior for the caregiver.

What you will find, of course, is that when you give patients the responsibility for their disease, they begin to change in many small ways. They will start to confront the disease, whereas before they may have used you, manipulated you, worn you out, let you make all the decisions and do all the work. If you're not doing it anymore, they will have to change.

Now they may get angry in the beginning. But ultimately, I believe, they will thank you. Understand that if you can listen to the people with the affliction, you will be helping. So learn how to listen—not manipulate, not control, not do—and they will have to make decisions and do things that will make your job easier.

This will allow you to take care of yourself and to have all the appropriate feelings, which may include anger at the other person, and fatigue. Don't consider yourself abnormal for being angry at somebody in your family who is sick. I feel this sometimes. If I love someone I can be upset with them for being sick. It makes their life and my life harder. I can get tired. But I still love them—I just don't like what's going on.

Share all that. Keep it out in the open and let the relationship grow, and when you are tired, take care of yourself. You have needs, too.

Sometimes I am asked, "Is there a way to help someone who doesn't want to be helped?" And the answer is that you can't help someone who doesn't want to be helped. But you can love that person and create a safe environment so that he or she will be capable of change. So you can support someone, and in that way that person may open to further help and change.

There are mechanical ways in which you can help a family member and still avoid guilt, such as giving books and tapes that the relative can look at, listen to, even dispose of. Your family member will know that you care and that you have provided a resource that he or she doesn't have to use. I have sometimes suggested getting family members into a car. When you're driving at fifty-five miles an hour you can put on a tape that you think might be a resource for them. They're unlikely to jump out of the car, and they will probably listen to the tape. They might not do what is expressed, but on the other hand it still gives you something to talk about, and change may occur slowly.

Take them to a lecture if they'll go with you. Or to a workshop. Again, they don't have to agree, but it gives you something to disagree about. And I mean that on friendly terms—something to talk about. It helps to open communication when none may have existed before.

How do you deal with the sadness of seeing people you love in pain, who do not have the strength to change? Again, I don't judge people or turn them into failures. I'm not forcing somebody to change. I'm offering paths and opportunities. How do you deal with the sadness? You express it, cry about it, maybe even in front of the person. Seeing the tears in your eyes and how much you care might get them to change.

Practical Problems

Families can feel overwhelmed by the enormous problems they encounter when cancer strikes: lack of money, home-care needs not covered by insurance, trying to handle everything while working at being available for the patient. These problems are not easily solved. But on one level I'd ask you to act up politically. Change the laws. Confront insurance companies. Confront the government. Use lawyers. Let's help people who are not adequately cared for. Why do we have to have nothing in order to receive help from the state? Why can't insurance be appropriately written and adjusted and all of us cared for in the event of catastrophes? As part of an insurance plan we could also find ways to reward people who help keep themselves healthy. Industry is beginning to change, seeing the advantage of health and that it is cost-effective. So be active, speak up, empower yourself. Changes are coming.

On a personal level, you can't be the only one to care for a loved one. Ask for help. Talk to the family. Assert yourself. Sometimes the ill person can be the one to do this for the family.

I think of the social worker who wrote to all of his friends saying, "I'm going to need all of you. All of you who get this letter are listed in the letter. You're to get together, have a meeting, work out a schedule so that I can get all the help I need, for trips, visits, shopping." And he created a family that has a party every year now based on that letter.

Don't be afraid to reach out. One lady told me, "Cab drivers helped and prayed for me; a veterinarian took care of my cat without charging me when they knew my husband had cancer."

Let people know. Be assertive. I see this at our work-shops. We let it be known that scholarships are available. If you want to come to a workshop and you don't have the money, call up and say, "I don't have the money, but I really want to be there." Believe me, if you talk to me or to the people running the workshop, the odds are that you will be there. Maybe we'll ask you to be a volunteer or to help in some way, but you'll be there.

When things really get difficult, all I can say is, ask for help. Ask a professional. Ask social workers at the hospital, the organizations and societies, your local church or synagogue—any group. Let the community know. We had in our group a woman who couldn't afford to keep her apartment. The state wanted to move her to a cheaper apartment, farther from the hospital. It would have cost more to transport her to the hospital than the rent spent in the first apartment. I wrote to the state to explain that it would cost more. A newspaper article was written about the woman, donations came in to help her pay her rent, and between the state's changing its mind and people assisting her, she was able to remain in the same apartment. So don't be afraid to fight.

Life is difficult. Think of breaking up the difficulties into small pieces, small steps. And share the difficulties— then they may become bearable. The secret is learning to live with and to use the difficulties one encounters.

Nothing Is Impossible;
I Believe in Miracles

If I get a telephone call asking if it is possible to reverse Alzheimer's, or autism, or any other disease, my answer is, if I know someone who's done it, "Yes." Otherwise I say, "Do you want to try?" That is the real issue.

There are people who have stayed quite well with a diagnosis of Alzheimer's. I know from families who have put in incredible amounts of attention and care and touch that some individuals have done amazingly well. And if you want to try to reverse the disease, fine.

Look into all the nutritional, emotional, psychological and medical things that you can—traditional and alternative—and see what can be accomplished. Even if it's just from the aspect of hope, it is worth trying. Guilt can enter if you don't try, or if you don't cure the disease. If guilt is a part of your pattern, then look it in the eye and become a winner by your effort, and not by the outcome alone. Make what efforts feel right for you in confronting any disease. I don't care what the disease is.

If you're dealing with someone who is brain-injured and you are told that there is no chance of recovery, again I say don't accept a verdict or a sentence. Keep communicating, sharing, talking, making tapes, playing music, talking to the individual. It's surprising what has happened to people in terms of recovery from brain injury. People who are blind have learned to see again. People who were told they were never going to accomplish anything have gone to college. We can relearn and retrain.

If you're going to feel guilty if a miracle doesn't occur, then don't try. But if you say, "This is my child, my loved one, and I want to see what I can accomplish," then by all means give 'em hell, do all you can, and see what transpires.

Take on the challenge. Look at it. Say, "Examine me, Oh Lord, and Try me." That's with a capital T.

I received a letter from a woman whose uncle had cancer of the liver and pancreas; she felt that the doctors had basically "written him off." She said, "I need you to tell me what to do for Uncle Charles."

My response is, remember to ask Uncle Charles

what he needs or wants. Don't turn your family members into failures, but just love your uncle and be with him and support him. Can you find options for Uncle Charles? Sure, even if they're only a hope and a prayer. Can you ask him what he would like to do? Yes. Can you introduce him to other people who are fighters and survivors and unique, exceptional individuals? Yes. And that will help him to live. It isn't that we don't die or that Uncle Charles might not die, but he will have lived before he died, and everybody will be left with a gift from him and will be proud of him, as he will be of himself. He will have beaten cancer.

A gentleman named Peter Uhlman wrote to Bobbie and me thanking us for helping him and his wife "beat cancer": "I thank you for empowering us with knowledge and strength. In our humor we healed our lives and in the process we beat cancer."

How could someone beat cancer? Stop and think about it for a moment. My answer is that beating cancer relates to how you live, not to living forever. Peter Uhlman went on to say that after his wife's prognosis:

> The doctors sent her home five days later to die.
>
> We packed the car and went in search of second opinions; it was a trip we deemed "Cancer Tour '92." We stopped just shy of getting shirts printed. We learned a lot about what was wrong with the medical profession in the next few days. We were told at one place that we didn't have the "right attitude," that this was serious and that we should not be laughing. We were even told by a doctor that we had a total "irreverence" for this disease. We took it as a compliment.
>
> As Diane got sicker we clung to all the things we had learned earlier from "Bernie." We mended relationships, embraced life, planned our future,

laughed, prayed, cried and dreamed together. The
one thing we learned is that cancer is not only a
physical disease but it is a metaphorical disease,
and we would not let cancer metastasize to our
marriage.

Diane died as I sang to her in the evening,
seven weeks after she had been diagnosed. All my
life I have been so scared of death. I have spent a
lot of time trying to distinguish whether I truly love
life or if I really just hate death; there is a big difference. I had to tell my wife it was okay to let go,
that I would continue on, you know, pay the taxes,
feed the cat, care for her mom. We were still making jokes with each other an hour before she died.
My wife in her last act of love liberated me from
this fear, and gave me peace of mind.

They truly did beat cancer.

6
"In Love's Service": The Healing Professions

Not every patient can be saved, but his illness may be eased by the way the doctor responds to him—and in responding to him the doctor may save himself. But first he must become a student again; he has to dissect the cadaver of his professional persona; he must see that his silence and neutrality are unnatural. It may be necessary to give up some of his authority in exchange for his humanity, but as the old family doctors knew, this is not a bad bargain. In learning to talk to his patients, the doctor may talk himself back into loving his work. He has little to lose and everything to gain by letting the sick man into his heart.

If he does, they can share, as few others can, the wonder, terror, and exaltation of being on the edge of being, between the natural and the supernatural.

—ANATOLE BROYARD
INTOXICATED BY MY ILLNESS

Changing the Way
Doctors Are Trained

When I am asked how I would change medical education, I think of a wonderful painting called "The Doctor," now in the Tate Gallery in London. Stop for a
minute, and think about it. If I asked you to do a painting called "The Doctor," what would you portray?
There are many paintings by that name, and they illus-
trate different scenes. The one I am thinking of shows
a man sitting in a cabin, leaning over the bed of a sick
child. He is not surrounded by fancy equipment; he is
just listening and caring while the concerned parents
are in the background. The artist, Sir Luke Fildes,
painted this picture in 1891. He had the experience of
having one of his children die, on Christmas Day. He
knows what "the doctor" means to him. Today if I said
to a group of doctors, "Please paint a picture called
'The Doctor,'" it might just be filled with instruments
and white coats.

When I show a slide of this painting I ask people to tell me if it is called "Too Late" or "The Doctor." People can feel the care in the painting, and they call it "The Doctor." I want physicians to understand that it is never too late, that there is always someone in need of healing. We must remember that the word **doctor** has as its root meaning "to teach."

Over my desk at home and in the office I have hung copies of the Fildes painting—to remind myself about the kind of physician I wanted to be, and that it is never too late to teach and to heal.

Certainly doctors and nurses do not set out to build walls around themselves or to be villains. If you go to a medical school graduation you don't get mad at the hundreds of young men and women who are graduating and looking forward to helping people. The problem is what happens to them in their training and in the ensuing years. The pain of life and the pain of the people they're caring for begin to affect them more and more, and they stop feeling, because they have no guidance. One doctor wrote he felt doctors were like diners feeding the same slop to the same customers over and over again, each hating the other. Medical schools need to teach doctors that it is important to express feelings and to share the difficulties of being a doctor through meetings and classes in which they can talk to one another about their pain.

I think it is our training that is villainous. Even when medical students go into training, they are not given the support and education they need to keep from depersonalizing people. Some of that is obviously due to the people teaching them, who haven't themselves dealt with those issues. But unless we empower the students and the patients to speak up and demand what is needed, change is going to be slow. What the present system will create is a group of people who might have been excellent physicians who no longer choose to be physicians, or who may have to be very careful in the specialties they select so they can protect themselves. Most physicians would not be physicians again, nor want their children to become physicians, and others are becoming so specialized that medical care will be affected adversely. Certain specialties remove you from caring for truly sick people who might threaten you or make you feel inadequate.

There are a lot of ways in which I would like to "humanize" medical education. I would insist that doctors experience what it is like to be ill themselves. I'd like to see each doctor put into a hospital where he or she is not known, with a diagnosis of a life-threatening illness. He or she would stay there for a week and see how such patients are treated.

I would like the doctors to be treated in a way that will lead them to be "natives," so that they will be able to say to a patient, "I have some understanding of what you're going through. I have experienced this too."

Patients should become part of the training process. Physicians would learn that they are treating people, not only diseases, and that people are different from textbook cases. I'd introduce them to people during the first week of medical school, not just to a textbook or a dead body, but to a living human being. I'd encourage patients to say, "Here I am, and I want you to know what it's like to be sick. I want you to know why you're studying all this."

Medical students and doctors who have had cancer, AIDS and other life-threatening illnesses should speak to future doctors. Doctors should hear about dreams and drawings, about the work of Carl Jung and others, all of which tap into the knowledge of patients. I'd have ninety-year-olds give lectures. This is done at some schools, so that doctors can better understand the experience of living.

Doctors should attend sessions at shrines such as Lourdes where incurables come, so that they will understand the value of hope and prayer. How do we give hope? How do we show the value of prayer? What good is your medical education at a shrine, where all the people are incurable? Well, you begin to realize that what is valuable is your presence. If we worked in nursing homes, in hospice care, we would refocus on the care of the patient. We need to be exposed to things that we can't cure, so that we learn how to care for people and how to deal with feelings of failure and guilt. A patient initially doing well told his doctor that he had one thousand people praying for him. When his disease recurred, the doctor said, "Maybe you should have had two thousand." Is that caring?

One doctor wrote to me about his experience since having carcinoma. He and his wife have begun taking ballroom dancing lessons, they have appeared in a theater production, attended a local cancer support group, taken up sketching lessons. He has started to live. But he also says that other physicians have tended to avoid him. Only one of the four doctors in his synagogue visited him and spoke with him about his surgery. That is another problem for doctors—we don't visit because we are afraid of our feelings, our vulnerability. Behind the desk you are safe. Put your desk against the wall and be open to your patients!

I would teach doctors how to communicate. How do you tell patients they have AIDS or cancer without taking their hope away? How do you help them keep their power? The permission slips, the protocols that we ask patients to sign are destructive. No one has taught us how to word them so that people are not induced into negative beliefs and side effects.

While our son Stephen was in college, he painted an interesting picture; basically it consists of the word **words**. Take a pen or a pencil, repeat **words** several times without a space between the letters, and you will see that the words turn into swords: WORDS-WORDSWORDS. In the center of Stephen's painting it says: "signifying nothing." Well, of course, it does signify something: Words can be incredibly destructive. In the middle of the swords there is a word.

Physicians need to learn that (s)words like **poison, blast, attack, kill, assault** and **insult** are destructive when taken in both at a conscious and unconscious level. Bobbie and I wrote an article called "War and Peace" just to focus on how doctors look at disease and the war we fight with disease.

It isn't just our medications and operations that have an impact; words can also cure or kill. In one meeting I had with Norman Cousins, he used the term **psychological malpractice**. And the psychiatrist Milton Erikson used the term **iatrogenic health**. We often talk about iatrogenic disease, which is the disease that is induced by the medical treatment. But we could induce health and avoid psychological malpractice. Doctors can actually shorten an individual's life by what they say, when they take hope away.

We could encourage medical schools to introduce courses—some are already doing so—in which doctors learn to talk to people about their fears, so that we don't learn only facts in the first two years. As the schools open this door they make it permissible for us to talk about our problems, and we realize that we are not weak. When you go to a medical school and talk with the faculty, they speak of the "hard" subjects and the "soft" subjects. Well, who wants to be a softie? The soft subjects concern people. How do you prove it's valuable to learn how to take care of people? Those who teach the "hard" subjects can give a test to prove that a student knows the facts. But the results of the "soft" subjects show up only later, with the peace of mind of patients, with people leaving the hospital sooner, healing faster, suing less frequently—results that are not going to appear on an exam.

A physician at the University of California at Irvine started a course called "The Soft Subjects and Caring for People." As an orthopedic surgeon in Vietnam he had been caring for a soldier who had fractured his leg in a helicopter crash. The doctor put on a cast, but the man's pain was terrible. So he took the cast off, thinking it had not been put on properly; he replaced it, and still the pain was incredible. Each time he changed the cast he talked with the young man, who eventually revealed that all his buddies had died in the crash and he was feeling guilty that he had survived. When the young man had finished his story, the pain went away. The surgeon came back from Vietnam realizing how much of one's life and one's pain are related to what is going on emotionally. And so he started this course for his students to help them understand that within the "soft subjects" there is a lot of science and a lot about pain and healing.

I see changes today that make me feel hopeful. As I look back at brochures from the American Cancer Society from the 1980s, they were talking about cancer, not people; they were telling people not to rely on self-induced healing, as it was unproven scientifically. But self-induced healing is the only kind of healing there is. I wrote to the American College of Surgeons about their pledge, which includes the words "I will **deal** with my patients as I would wish to be **dealt** with if I were in the patient's position." I don't want to be "dealt with"— I want to be cared for and cared about. I may add that they responded to my letter and have invited me to write an article. However, they have not printed it two months later. The American Cancer Society is also doing the kinds of psycho–social training for doctors and nurses that it was looking down upon years ago.

I do think that doctors are becoming more open to many of these ideas now. I get more and more calls from medical schools, hospitals, and medical organizations, asking me to come and speak. Doctors who ten or fifteen years ago wondered why I was invited to come to their institutions are now introducing me. They are becoming more open because they are beginning to understand their own pain and that of their patients.

A friend of ours who is now a radiation oncologist, Matt Mumber, started a group called GEMS ("Group of Exceptional Medical Students") at the University of Virginia Medical School. At first it was hard for the students to know who should join—did you have to have all A's? But Matt made it clear that membership was related to compassion, love and healing. It became a recognized extracurricular activity at the school. The students met regularly to deal with the topics mentioned above and their feelings related to them. Matt, drawing himself as an oncologist, family doctor and surgeon, helped him decide on his specialty.

The Wounded Healer

In an essay entitled "The Religio–Psychological Dimension of the Wounded Healers," Dr. James Knight talks about Thornton Wilder's play "The Angel That Troubled the Waters." In the play a physician comes periodically to the Pool of Bethesda; it is believed that healing will occur there whenever an angel troubles the waters. The physician

> . . . waits for the angel, hoping to be the first in the pool and to be healed of his melancholy and remorse. The angel appears, but blocks the physician as he is ready to step into the water and be healed. . . The physician pleads, but the angel insists that healing is not for him; and then come these telling words from the angel:
> "Without your wound where would your power be? It is your melancholy that makes your low voice tremble into the hearts of men. The very angels themselves cannot persuade the wretched and blun-

dering children on earth as can one human being broken on the wheels of living. In love's service only the wounded soldiers can serve. Draw back."

Later, the person who was healed rejoiced in his good fortune and turned to the physician before leaving the pool of Bethesda and said, "But come with me first, an hour only, to my home. My son is lost in dark thoughts. I—I do not understand him, and only you have ever lifted his mood. Only an hour. . . My daughter, since her child has died, sits in the shadow. She will not listen to us. . . but she will listen to you."

Because of my own pain, I became more sensitive to the pain of others. It was my wounds that led me to workshops. And of course the reason I am writing this book is because of the patient I sat next to at a workshop; she was also in pain, and we both needed to know how to live. Doctors are called "attending physicians," and in a sense we need to attend to **our** wounds as well as to the wounds of others. We can help one another in the healing process. Please do not hide your wounds.

The Doctor and the Patient

Originally medical care incorporated three entities: preaching, teaching and healing. When I say preaching, I mean that doctors helped people find their inner strength and spirituality. They helped heal lives, and they cured diseases as well. Along the way preachers have taken over one role, teachers another, and doctors have become mechanics. I think we need to bring all of these professions together. Professionals are in pain when they are limited in this way.

In the Jewish religion, an interpretation of the treatment of disease free of guilt comes from Maimonides, who said that the basis of the permission to interfere is the commandment in Deuteronomy to restore lost objects. This is repeated more than once in the Bible, according to Rabbi David Feldman in his book *Health and Medicine in the Jewish Tradition*:

> If you find a book, money, fruit, it belongs to some-body else. You can't just wait for the person to come and collect it. You have to announce it actively, aggressively, you have to go about in the marketplace and say, "I have found a lost object, whoever can identify it, please come and get it." Maimonides said that is how we know the doctor may and must heal. He is restoring lost health. If a person has lost his health, the doctor, nurse and medical staff with the necessary skills are able to retrieve what he has lost and therefore they have an obligation to do so.

When you think of illness in this way—versus God wanting you to be sick, or of cancer as a punishment for something you have done—you can see how much healthier this approach is and how God becomes a resource. Physicians need to know something about religion so they can help people deal with illness in the context of their own religion. And that includes citing the Bible, and being aware of the issue of guilt. The words **pain** and **punishment** have the same root.

In a speech composed (but never delivered) by the late Andre E. Hellegers, he said:

> As the caring branches of medicine were gradually pushed aside by the curing ones, there seem to be less use for the Christian virtues. I think that shortly the need for those old Christian virtues will return and once again be at a premium. Our patients will need a helping hand and not a helping knife. This is no time to dismantle the low technol-

ogy care model of medicine. We must either cap-
ture the Christian virtues of care or we shall be
screaming to be induced into death to reach the
discomfort-free society.

I would use the term **spiritual virtues**, rather than
Christian virtues. But perhaps what he describes has
happened already. When *Final Exit*, a book about how
to commit suicide, becomes a bestseller, this says much
about being induced into death.

Dr. Deepak Chopra, physician and author, discusses in his book *The Return of the Rishi: The Doctor's Search for the Ultimate Healing* being called when
he was an intern to see a man who had died; he had to
pronounce the man dead and share that with the family. Everything had been medically proper, he said, but
so unhealthy:

> . . . The machines were in the room and the family
> was outside the door. That seemed peculiar to me.
> In India, the family is in the room and the
> machines are nowhere.

He goes on to say that many people now believe
the system of American medicine needs improvement,
perhaps a drastic overhauling. After two years, he
thought that he understood The System—it consisted
of thousands of hospitals and hundreds of thousands
of doctors. But:

> . . . If you break it down into its basic unit, the
> medical system is just a doctor and a patient, just
> two people. And they need to have a personal
> exchange, with the doctor playing one part and the
> patient the other. If the exchange turns out well,
> you have the practice of medicine. If it turns out
> badly, you have problems.

Dr. Chopra discusses his reaction to a patient: "We were bound by emotions that lie beyond personality. We were bound by love. A patient occupies a privileged position in my life that nothing else can explain."

Profound feelings occur, Dr. Chopra says, only when the physician is totally willing to accept his responsibility. If there is any fear of disease, any rejection of the patient, or any clinging to authority, then conventional medicine cannot become what should be an art; it remains a common trade:

> More and more I believe that the transcending can happen because I have come to feel when I am face to face with patients, that I am them. I lose the sense that we are separate. We are not. I can feel their pain as they describe it. I can understand them without blame, and want them to get well because I will be getting well myself.

Carl Jung spoke about how the doctor must learn the patient's story. In *Memories, Dreams, Reflections* he wrote:

> Clinical diagnoses are important since they give the doctor a certain orientation; but they do not help the patient. The crucial thing is the story. For it alone shows the human background and the human suffering, and only at that point can the doctor's therapy begin to operate.

The story is the patient's metaphor. The metaphor can help you see inside an individual; it can help you gently cut through to what is actually significant for him or her. By entering in this way you enter into the sacred space of the individual you're trying to help. You're not just staying on the outside, writing prescriptions; rather, like a war buddy, you are entering into the heat of the battle and the sacredness of that individual's life.

Learning from Patients

I began to realize years ago that our greatest resource is the people we take care of. When I started as an intern, many nurses and patients told me how to be a better doctor. I assumed they were doing that for everyone, but later I realized that they weren't. And now I ask young physicians, "Has a nurse or patient ever told you how to be a better doctor?" If they say yes, they already are better doctors, because they are open and vulnerable, and patients are not afraid to speak to them and question them and even be critical.

Please, doctors, be open to your patients. Be there when a patient dies. Be with families. Let them sustain you. Deliver eulogies at funerals. I have done this, because people have asked me to share their lives, to tell stories about life. This has made me confront my own mortality, my own death, and then I had the courage to be present and to share my vulnerability. That's what I would say to every physician: Deal with your mortality, your death, your humanity, and your actions will help you become a true healer.

A woman who is incarcerated in a criminal justice system wrote me to say that when she arrived there, she was diagnosed as HIV positive. She read my books and listened to meditation tapes, and felt that they helped her. A few months later she decided to be retested. The doctor called her into her office, saying that her test was uncertain and that she wanted to do another test.

Little did I know that the test had come back negative and she couldn't believe it. So she took more blood and sent it off. A week later she called me back to tell me I was HIV negative and that the previous test had been negative also. She and I cried a lot. She said that either the first test was a false positive, or that a miracle had happened in my life. I choose to believe the latter.

The point I want to make about this letter is that the doctor had a wonderful response of crying with her but then went back to being the typical doctor. "You've had either a false positive or a miracle." Why couldn't she say instead, "You may have had a false positive, you may have had a miracle, but maybe you did something I should learn about. Will you tell me about it?" The woman could have discussed her lifestyle changes and taught the doctor something to be passed on to others. We doctors keep saying things like, "You're lucky," or "You've had a spontaneous remission." Let us learn from these people who have exceeded expectations.

Such cases have been documented. The Institute of Noetic Sciences is publishing a collection of more than 4,000 cases ranging from spontaneous remissions to healings of a spiritual nature, so that these will be accessible to physicians and to the public. And look at the future evolution and potential of the body as described in Michael Murphy's book *The Future of the Body*. He reviews some of the documented extraordinary phenomena human beings are capable of.

I have worked with enough people to know that there is an awareness in the mind about what is happening in the body. I know people who are aware of their own blood count, who can control it, who when told by an oncologist that their count is too high and they need more chemotherapy have said, "No, I am in charge of my blood count. If you want it lower, I'll be happy to make it lower." They leave the office, go home and work on it, and come back with the count that makes the oncologist happy. We ought to be open to this awareness and use it. Physicians are probably the hardest ones to convince, because this is not a part of our experience or our training.

Learning from Your Experience

We can also be our own teachers. We don't have to learn only from others. There are times we can pick up our own torch, and as we light our way we also light the path for others, doctors as well as patients.

I want to share the pain of a conscientious physician who wrote me to say: "I missed a diagnosis and it appears the patient is going to die. I have given myself the flu to take time out to deal with my feelings."

This is a doctor who has been in practice for many years and missed diagnosing a carcinoma of the colon, even though her initial workup was quite proper and all the tests were done. And so the symptoms were considered to be due to irritable bowel until later tests showed metastatic cancer in the liver. She continued:

> I am partly afraid to go back to work, which I must do tomorrow, for fear of hurting someone else by errors of omission. I'm more aware than ever of the huge responsibility of being a physician and suddenly not sure I want it. And yet when things are going well I love my work and feel I have been blessed with the ability to help others. My questions are, How does one live with mistakes that cost people their lives? How do you personally deal with the responsibility of being a doctor? How do I forgive myself and carry on?

I think that in a sense this entire book is an answer to her, but I also know that one must see one's human-

ity and fallibility not as a sign of failure but simply as a
sign of being human. Obviously I think each physician
should be a good mechanic and know his or her subject and material. We are human, and we also need to
forgive ourselves when we are not perfect. But most of
all, I'd say that healing needs to go on between the
patient and the physician. We forgive each other when
we admit our humanity, but we don't forgive each
other when we try to play God and feel that we should
be perfect.

If this doctor had gone to the patient and shared
with the patient what she shared with me, a great deal
of healing might have gone on for her. What if this letter describing how she felt had been written to the
patient? I dare say she'd receive a letter back from the
patient saying, "Please, doctor, I know you cared and it
isn't your fault. Please continue to help others and don't
stop being a doctor. If you hadn't cared, I wouldn't
want you for my doctor." But when we are afraid and
withdraw and act mechanistic and stop feeling and only
think, that's when we die inside, when lawsuits occur
and conflict results. We need to listen to each other and
share the pain, and then healing can happen.

Another doctor asked, "How do you deal with grief
as a professional, remain effective and helpful to your
patients and their families without feeling torn up?
How do you survive being a doctor, with all of the
pain, responsibility and guilt?"

The answer is, with difficulty. As a doctor you have
dreams about the operations you're going to perform
because you're worried about doing them properly. You
feel pain when beautiful people die. You feel torn apart
in the operating room when you can't cure cancer, when
you can't remove it. Through it all you begin to awaken
to a realization that you have something more to offer
people—you can stay with them, hold their hand.

You can help them to live during the time that they
have.

Giving support, loving and caring, not deserting someone—that's what gets you through. And you get back an enormous gift, the love of many incredibly courageous people who teach you to stop fearing and to stop being angry and resenting and to simply know that difficulties are inherent in life.

Robert E. Murphy, a third-year student, wrote an essay called "First Day" for the *Journal of the American Medical Association* about his first experience in the coronary care unit. It was horrendous. The resident said, "Quit now—it just gets worse." He said he felt more and more stupid as the day wore on. He was not able to answer questions—they weren't multiple choice. The nurses were constantly after him with more questions. He didn't find time for lunch. And finally, "I was told to stick Mr. Hunt for cardiac enzymes. I had only drawn blood on three classmates (and missed one of those)." Whenever I tell this story I stop at that point and ask, "What's different about this?" Notice that he "sticks" Mr. Hunt but "draws blood on" classmates. He is depersonalizing the patient already. Murphy goes on, "I palpated a nice vein in his left arm and was ready to stick him when he said, 'You know, I don't think you're supposed to draw that above the IV.' Even the patients knew more than I did."

But because of his difficulties drawing the blood, trying three times and not getting any, he and Mr. Hunt had a chance to talk, and he explained to Mr. Hunt all of the reasons he was in the hospital and the nature of the tests they were doing. And in the end, because of the trouble he was having, he said he would get the intern. Mr. Hunt said, "Naw, give it another shot. I know you can do it." And he did. When he was about to leave, Mr. Hunt commented, "You're one of those student doctors, aren't you?" He nodded and confessed that Mr. Hunt was his first patient. Mr. Hunt said, "Nobody has sat down and said a word to me for two days. I know you're real smart and you're a mighty nice fella. You're gonna be a good doctor, I can tell." Murphy finished the story with, "It was a very good first day."

I know physicians who do talk to patients and are penalized for taking so much time by having their salaries cut. Speak up as patients. Help change the system.

I realized in the same way in my own practice that I could say to patients, "I'm having a lousy day." And that included patients lying in the intensive-care unit on respirators. I remember with great emotion going to see a woman in her twenties—she was a nurse with extensive cancer that had spread to her lungs. The only way she could breathe was on a respirator. I went because the family wanted me to help her. I didn't know what I could offer her. And when I walked into the room and she saw me, she sat up, put her arms out, and embraced me. She really took care of me. From then on, I had no fear of ever visiting anyone again, because I knew that we could give to each other, and we could hurt and suffer together.

Virginia Schafer, a nurse who spends twelve hours a day working in the hospital's emergency room and in the intensive-care unit, wrote to me about something that I had mentioned at a workshop. A mother had shared with me the fact that her child died after an auto accident. While she kept questioning the staff they wouldn't tell her that her child was dying, wouldn't allow her to be at the bedside, and when she went to see the neurosurgeon to tell him her feeling about the treatment, he charged her $50 for the office visit. Virginia Schafer said in her letter that it is extremely difficult to deal with an emotional parent in an emotionally charged situation:

> We are not insensitive jerks who are being mean keeping the mother away from her child. We are only humans trying to keep her child alive, setting

ourselves up for an emotional trauma of our own
as well as putting our legal butts on the line. I have
often been the object of anger because there was
no place else for people to direct it. I also have the
gift of being able to feel much of a mother's, or
spouse's, or child's pain.

She was upset with me for not presenting both
sides of the argument, so to speak. But the point I want
to make is that just as she is feeling the pain probably
far more than most physicians or nurses (or she
wouldn't have responded to the story as she did), what
we need to do is to let one another know our needs.
The listening and the communicating are the healing.
We can't cure each other's problems. But we can care
for one another, and I think if care had been extended
to that mother, or if she had been told what this nurse
put in the letter to me—that this is painful for us, too,
that we are trying to save your child's life—then that
mother would have felt differently.

In Arthur Miller's play *Death of a Salesman*, Willie
Loman's wife, Linda, says of him:

> I don't say he's a great man. . . But he's a human
> being, and a terrible thing is happening to him. So
> attention must be paid. He's not to be allowed to
> fall into his grave like an old dog. Attention, atten-
> tion must be finally paid to such a person.

Do we "attending physicians" pay attention, do we
listen, do we attend to the needs of others? When we
can help other human beings face their mortality and
end their lives in a blaze of glory rather than falling
into their graves like old dogs, we have done something real, and we have accomplished something. I
read this to a meeting of veternarians. Even old dogs
shouldn't die without attention for themselves and
their grieving owners.

When we change our view of our role as health care providers of all kinds and are not victims of our profession, we can become true healers and not burn out.

Burning Up, Not Burning Out

One of the keys to "burning up" rather than burning out is to bring more of yourself into your work. Don't try to conform to some inner idea of the role of "doctor." That is exhausting. Be yourself. This means taking care of yourself as well as of your patients—live what you preach, and find support for yourself.

A doctor wrote to me most eloquently about the pressures and challenges he was feeling:

> How does a doctor balance the demands of full-time medical practice with the need for self love and care? I've cut back and am still working 40–60 hours a week. I have trouble maintaining marriage, family, my patients' needs and my own. How do I keep from burning out?

You and I can keep from burning out by living our lives. You are where you want to be. You have choices. You are not a victim. Listen to that inner voice that helps guide you.

One night some years ago I was awakened at two in the morning by a phone call from the emergency room. I hung up and heard a voice—not my wife's—say, "I don't want to go to the emergency room." And another voice said, "But you're in Dr. Siegel's body, you have to go." And the two of them argued for a while and I thought I'd probably had a breakdown or become schizophrenic. The two agreed that because they were in Dr. Siegel's body they would go to the hospital, but that Dr. Siegel had to understand that if he didn't like being awakened at two in the morning and going to the E.R., he could stop being Dr. Siegel. And I suddenly realized that this was my choice. I was not a victim. There was no reason to be angry at the people in the emergency room—staff or patients. This experience freed me to be myself and to realize that I was in charge, and that I could stop if I didn't like what was happening.

Think about why you are a doctor. Sometimes people feel trapped. But you can realize: "I don't have to be a doctor." When you give yourself the freedom to do something else, then you're back in charge.

Once you realize that you are not trapped, you will stop being angry at those who you feel are forcing you to come to the emergency room, to be away from your family. You cannot be doctor, parent, husband or wife, friend, and on and on. Those are roles. You figure out who you are, and then live your life. And that can be shared with your family, obviously.

I realize that I chose being a surgeon because it offered me a way of fulfilling a lot of things I was interested in. Helping people, being inquisitive about science, liking to fix things, liking to work with my hands—all of these could be combined.

But if I like helping people, I've learned that being a doctor isn't the only path available to me. I can take care of and help people in many ways and still fulfill aspects of my personality. I could work in an elevator or serve sandwiches in our son's Subway franchise. Think about it: I can make sandwiches, cut them up, serve them by wearing gloves just as in the operating room and feel wonderful that I've helped people and have done a lot of the things that I enjoy doing as a surgeon. There is work I can do that has less morbidity and that will be joyful because I am relating to people.

I know of driving instructors, hairdressers, subway conductors and others who with a so-called trapped audience have changed people by giving them love.

One bus driver made a difference by giving out muffins and doughnuts on Monday mornings. He said, "I had to do something. I never saw so many miserable people in one place." I have seen a school custodian be asked to give the commencement address in high school because the seniors knew that he had a sense of humor and cared about them.

A doctor, Camille Schiano, has been complimented by the nurses for the way she deals with people. But, she said

> I fear I have become a flickering candle. Patients introduce themselves as educated consumers and inform me of their past history and lawsuits. Nice patients call me at all hours. More of my colleagues read *The Wall Street Journal* than other literature. I was feeling anxious, tired, frustrated and frightened, so I decided to change my career. I contemplated a position in parochial pastoral education, but no one would hire me. Then I attempted to obtain a position through the nursing department. There are several jobs in which I could use my talents. Well, I was rejected, since only nurses are hired for these jobs. I continue to search.

You don't have to become a member of the clergy or a nurse to care for people (or, as I thought, a veterinarian in order to hug your patients). It is how Dr. Schiano views the role of doctor that can be altered. As Bobbie stated years ago, I could be a "clergeon" and practice "clergery"—a combination of surgery and clergy work—and this doctor needs to understand that she can combine all of the things she is interested in and be the kind of physician she wants to be.

Once we define what our role really is, we can find happiness. But if your role is to cure people and not let them die, then you will feel like a failure.

Look at why you are doing what you're doing. Do

you still love being a doctor? If not, consider the ways in which you could change. Now if you say, "I want to accumulate enough money so I can give myself freedom," fine. Then you have a goal, and you are working toward it. But you may begin to realize that you don't need as much money as you thought in order to survive. We can reduce our need for money; we can find out how little we actually do need. And then you can include in your life some meditation, gardening, vacation, volunteer work, and other things that bring joy and restore you. Don't work for a living and then have no time left to live.

If you don't do what you love, that void is going to catch up with you some day. Stop. You'll survive. You'll make it. Believe me.

Life will restore your batteries and recharge your cells.

And if you **do** choose to remain a physician, the difficulties become your choice: dealing with the forms, the government, the operating room, the nurses and patients.

Don't try to be some label called "doctor." Be yourself. Share yourself with your patients. I think that this applies to any profession: see the people, relate to the people. Then it becomes joyful to practice.

Native Intelligence

You know what I mean by the term **native**, and we are all natives in one sense or another. When a doctor uses that basic native intelligence, healing can happen at another level.

There is a story in the January 8, 1992, *Journal of the American Medical Association* called "A Doctor in Her House," written by Bernadine Z. Paulshock, M.D., about another doctor. A physician went to visit and treat a sick mother whose children had chicken pox.

She gave advice to the mother and then left. The pediatrician came later to see the children. The next day when the first physician called, the mother said,

> Doctor M. did something really great for us. After he left he went over to the supermarket and brought back milk and juice and barbecued chicken and bananas. I was so surprised. He didn't even let me pay him. He really is one terrific doctor.

That is how we heal—in those small acts between one human being and another.

A woman shared an experience she had with her oncologist, describing how for her a simple act had enormous power. "He once tied my shoes after my treatment. Suddenly I felt like a human being."

When doctors become involved in their patients' lives they can cure in ways they may not expect. One doctor told about a woman and her child who had come to see him. He wrote some prescriptions for antibiotics and then asked, "What's going on in your life?" He learned that the woman's husband had left her. After listening for a while he realized that what she needed was to speak to Legal Aid. They spoke for a time and so he gave her the telephone number, and she forgot to pick up her prescriptions. When she came back a week later she was beaming and healthy, as was her child. The visit to Legal Aid had solved her problem. The antibiotics turned out to be unnecessary. Someone cared and responded, she felt hope, and she could go on.

The Gift of Hope

Hope is a wonderful resource for the physician. Even when things seem hopeless, to give a family hope is never wrong. I am not talking about lying, but about hope.

There are many people I know who were not given hope who are alive and well today because they had the strength to go on. A man who was diagnosed five years ago with AIDS wrote to share some good news. He had gone to his doctors to ask if they would give him AIDS antigen test. The doctors were at first reluctant, but he felt sure what the result would be, and asked them to humor him:

> . . . I finally got them to do it and the last test came back Negative, no evidence of viral activity. This was a wonderful confirmation for me of what you, Louise Hay [author and workshop leader] and others have been saying all along. The power of faith and conviction in knowing what is true for oneself regardless of what everyone else is telling you can indeed work miracles of healing. Thank you for your message of hope.

A doctor once said about me, "He's telling people what they want to hear." I've also had the criticism that I give "false hope." But there is no false hope. False hope tends to be a recital of statistics, and people are not statistics. But there is false "no hope." I don't think that the gentleman who had AIDS, even if he hadn't gotten well, would be writing to say, "Oh, you upset me by telling me what I wanted to hear." That's an absurdity. I am not telling lies, I am telling truths.

I am not denying the seriousness of many, many diseases. I expect to die some day, despite writing these books. What I am talking about is human potential and what may happen, and I can share that with people honestly and openly. It does not mean telling them what they want to hear; it means telling them that they have a chance to fight for their lives, that they're not sentenced to death. Some people want to hear it. Some don't want to take up the struggle. But to those who do want to fight for their lives, yes, it's what they want to hear—that there is a chance. There is for everybody. Doctors know that. But they get caught up in the mechanistic, statistical view of the world and stop seeing people. I see people because I talk to them, I read my mail, I meet people, and I know how wonderful they are and what they're capable of.

Hope isn't statistical, and individuals recover. There will always be a first person to recover from every disease.

I get many phone calls from people and families whose disease I can't cure and whom I can't help in a physical sense. But I listen, and at the end of my time of listening they feel stronger because they better understand their situation and the choices that are available to them.

When you the professional are dealing with the families of profoundly ill or disabled patients, be there for these people. Support them. Care for them, care about them. Call. Visit. It's a great gift to go into a home, see how courageous people are, and have them restore and heal you. A house call or a phone call may be for your sake, even more than for the family's sake.

Don't feel like a failure because you can't restore function or make every illness disappear. People need support. They will thank you profoundly for hope, they will thank you for your love, they will thank you for your humor.

Nobody gets angry at being given hope. I have never received a letter saying, "You made me laugh and gave me hope but I'm going to die anyway so I'm mad at you." I am stopped in hallways, airports, everywhere, by people who say, "Thank you." They will say, "My loved one died. But I want to thank you for what you brought into our lives."

The Hospital of the Future

Dr. Richard Selzer, my former surgical associate, reflects on the nature of the hospital in his book *Down from Troy: A Doctor Comes of Age*:

> The hospital differs from those ancient buildings in which living people were immured in that its house spirit enters the premises **after** it has been built and put into use. This spirit is born out of the suffering and death of those who occupy it. Year after year the building becomes re-created in the form of spirit as the suffering of the sick is set free within its walls.
>
> But what, you ask, has all this to do with the architecture of a hospital? All these fountains and wind chimes, the sacredness of brick, the vitality of wood, the house spirits—these are the fantasies of a mere scribbler who cannot even read blueprints. And I, in turn, ask: Where is the architect who, without sacrificing function and practicality, will think of the hospital as a pregnant woman who suffers the occupancy of a human being who enters, dwells for a time and ultimately passes forth? Where is the architect who, from the very moment he begins his design, will be aware that in each room of his finished hospital, someone will die? Who, while seated at his drawing board, will pause to feel upon his naked forearms the chill wind of his mortality? One day, he too will enter this building, not as its architect but as a supplicant in direst need. If I am wrong, and such human emotions cannot be expressed in architecture, why then it is time to surrender the hospital to writers, who will build it out of words and dreams.

What should a hospital of the future be like? The word **hospital** derives from **hospitality**. And for the benefit of both patients and staff, the hospital should become a more hospitable place. I'd like to see group meetings available in hospitals for nurses, for doctors, for aides and orderlies, so that they can communicate with one another and express their feelings and not take them out on the patients.

A hospital should have a meditation room, an exercise room and a resource room full of informative books and tapes—a "living room," I'd like to call it—so that the staff and the patients can go to those places to have peace and quiet, as well as information on healing and curing their afflictions.

In my training I was taught a lot about disease and about matter, but very little about the spirit. I can recall being led in prayer only once during my training, and that was just before an operation to separate "Siamese" twins. The prayer was led by Dr. William Kiesewetter of the Children's Hospital in Pittsburgh. He was a minister and a surgeon. I know how little, in a sense, spirituality fits into most hospitals and medical training. (I specifically use the word **spirituality** rather than **religion** because I know that religion can at times create guilt and be a handicap rather than an asset.)

A good-sized chapel would be lovely, not one hidden at the back door where no one can find it. I'd make spirituality a part of the institution and have a good chaplaincy staff available to patients.

When Yale New Haven Hospital was rebuilt several years ago, a chapel that had been near the front door was converted into a room half the size and placed at the back door, where it went unnoticed by most people. And in all the years I've sat there and meditated and prayed, I've never met another physician in that room, although I have found other members of the hospital staff. Praying with these people and being present with them in that setting helps enormously. Doing so helps unify the hospital, and, truthfully, if you pray with an X-ray technician it is hard to get angry at that technician if you have to wait a few extra minutes for an X-ray or if the machine doesn't work properly. You just have a different sense of life and of our being in this together. I believe that most physicians, because of this lack of training, do not have this added resource to draw on. (At this writing, Yale New Haven Hospital is building a children's hospital, and it is enlarging the chapel and introducing many things that were taken out years ago. I think the hospital is becoming aware, also, of the needs of the patients.)

There have been studies about the effect on patients when they are touched or worked on by a healer, versus people who have not been touched or treated by a healer. I have thought it would be a good idea to do a study in which people could send the names of their sick ones to prayer groups and see what would happen to the clinical course of that individual. I have presented this idea to some of the physicians I know, suggesting that we do a controlled study in which half of our patients were prayed for, but not the other half. The physicians wouldn't know which were prayed for and which were not, but we'd see at the end of the study who would go home sooner, who would need less pain medication, whose wounds would heal more quickly. But the general reaction from doctors has been "No." And I think it's "no" because they are uncomfortable with the concept, and if it did prove valid, maybe it would shake their foundations. I don't know. But we have to be willing to shake the foundations. If we're going to change the world, we have to be willing to look at the mysteries of the world—like any other group of scientists who aren't afraid to look at what they can't explain.

Anatole Broyard, who for many years wrote for the *New York Times*, did some especially meaningful writing when he developed prostate cancer. He said of the hospital:

To help the doctor reach the patient, and to help
the patient reach the doctor, the mood of the hospital might have to be modified. It ought to be less
like a laboratory and more like a theater, which
would only be fitting, since no place contains more
drama. The laboratory atmosphere can probably be
traced back to the idea of asepsis, to the avoidance
of contagion. Originally, the patient was protected
by the sterility of the hospital. Only the sterility
went too far: It sterilized the doctor's thinking. It
sterilized the patient's entire experience in the hospital. It sterilized the very notion of illness to the
point where we can't bring out soiled thoughts to
bear on it. But the sick man needs the contagion of
life.

In this spirit I would bring art and music into the
hospital, to help people deal with their fear, pain and
sorrow. And that includes children as well as adults. If
people want to participate, fine. If they don't, they
don't have to. But at least the services would be available.

Think about how much time is spent in waiting
rooms. Wouldn't it be lovely to be able to have a massage or guided imagery while waiting for therapy? You
could have earphones and a tape recorder, so that
when you sit waiting, you could deal with your anxi-
eties and focus on what will help you. In a recent
newsletter about the healing arts from The Institute for
the Advancement of Health, there is an article called
"The Medicine of Art," by Barbara Graham. She
describes some of what is happening in medical centers. For example, at Sloan Kettering Cancer Center in
New York City, music is being used to reduce pain.
Vietnam veterans in Louisville, Kentucky, are participating in a pilot project with sculpture, drawing and
music as a way of dealing with their stress disorder. Dr.

Joel Elkes, Director of the Arts in Medicine Program at the University of Louisville School of Medicine, says that in some way art appears to activate the healing system, and that in the future doctors may be prescribing art as therapy. Dr. Elkes and the school at Louisville are helping to change medical education by creating sensitive, caring students who turn out to be the same kind of physicians.

At other institutions music has been used and is actually available as a form of pain control versus traditional medications. Various TV channels are used in some centers to allow for the presentation of music and imagery, and I keep thinking how powerful a tool the closed-circuit TV is in every institution. It's there in the room. Why not bring in music, sound and images to help people heal, and for sharing and education? This would be far better than what I often see—people strapped down, on respirators, staring blankly at the news or at some horrendous soap opera that certainly doesn't inspire healing and that may even lead to more despair and depression. As Bobbie says, "Who wants to watch 'One Life to Live' while lying in the ICU?"

The TV could supply meditation, humor, healing— and thus would save enormous amounts of time for the nursing staff. People could see the treatments that they would be getting and examples of successful outcomes. There would be interviews with other patients with the same diseases, the same operations and procedures.

We are more and more aware of how sound can affect blood pressure, heart rate, immune response. I saw this years ago, because I brought healing music into the operating room—for my benefit and that of the nurses and the patients.

A study conducted at Yale showed that you can change electroencephalograms and relax people with the smell of apple-spice pie. Well, I keep thinking that if as you rolled into the operating room you smelled

coffee, apple-spice pie, heard soothing music, were surrounded by colors you like, and were touched gently,
you would know that this was a place of healing. We
could individualize the aromas, colors and sounds for
each patient.

These techniques don't all have to be used by the
same physician, but the physician who is aware of
them can guide the patient.

No one should have to say, "I was told I had cancer
and then the doctor left. No one came into my room to
tell me how to live with cancer." The American Cancer
Society in recent research has shown that by instituting
a six-week course to help people cope with cancer, the
patients had fewer recurrences and better survival
statistics, and Dr. David Spiegel's research supports this
concept as well. More of this research needs to be done.

I think we should have in the hospital an organization that responds when people are told that they have
cancer, AIDS or multiple sclerosis or that they need an
operation. Someone can come in, sit down and say,
"How are you doing? How do you feel? Can we help
you cope with the situation? What questions do you
have?" so that we don't just desert people. Nurses tell
me that they see doctors perform a biopsy, learn the
person has cancer, sit in the locker room for forty-five
minutes to pull themselves together, then go out and
brusquely say, "You have cancer" and walk away.

What do I say? Go spend the forty-five minutes sitting **with** the patient. Suffer together with the patient
and express your feelings. Patients need to have someone who is there for them when they learn of these
catastrophic events, not someone who will walk out
and leave them sitting in a room wondering where
their lives are going.

Many years ago I was told that a member of my
family had a very serious, progressive, untreatable illness. I was told this in the cafeteria of the hospital. The

doctor sat opposite me at the table and gave me the news. What was I supposed to do there, in the middle of the cafeteria? Cry, laugh, talk, respond? I thought, how ridiculous this is, and how angry I am. This person was protecting himself and being insensitive to my needs and my family's needs. I had to learn the hard way how to deal with that. That family member is well today, and all the fearful thoughts that went through my head never happened. But I became a native very quickly. I also realized that that physician was not trying to be cruel—he just did not understand.

But it would have been wonderful if somebody had come in at that moment, sat down with me and said, "Look, this is an insensitive clod who doesn't know how to deal with you. It's **his** problem. He has not been trained properly. He is a tourist. Now, how are you feeling? Let me introduce you to other natives with the same problem. Understand that we don't know the future, nor do you." My hope could have been restored. Instead I had to struggle with how to express myself, how to talk to the family. Let me tell you, I was terrible at it because I tried to be the strong one and carry this burden for my family. I became worn out and tired of deceiving people and making excuses. And so I learned that it was important to share, because everyone else was capable of dealing with it, and then supporting me.

Let's have people trained to help us. Let's have all the support services available to us—not just mechanical ones, but "humanity services" that will help us as human beings.

Hospitals should not only treat disease but should teach people how to live, how to support and sustain themselves, so that when people leave the hospital they have learned something about themselves and how to go on living. When they get back out into the world again, they may say that hospitalization was a gift because of what it taught them.

7
Reflections: Spirituality, Religion and Healing

. . . a prominent Russian scientist, a special-
ist in the chemistry of the brain, discovered
religion as an adult and. . . was interviewed
about how a scientist could suddenly accept
religion. He said among other things, "I
remember the first time I tried to pray, to
probe the depths of my heart and reach
God. My scientific mind said to me, 'You
fool, what are you doing? To whom do you
think you're speaking?' To this day, I have
a great fear about what would have hap-
pened to me if I had not overcome my intel-
lectual hesitation at that moment."

In a Hassidic story, the disciple comes to
the rabbi and says, "I have a terrible prob-
lem. I can't pray. I try to say the words but
nothing happens. I don't feel anything.
What should I do?" The rabbi answers,
"Pray for the ability to pray."

—HAROLD KUSHNER
WHO NEEDS GOD?

The Role of a Spiritual
Life in Healing

I was brought up in the Jewish tradition and grew up believing that God restores us and sustains us, that God is a resource. If I lose my health, then God is there to assist me in restoring my health and supporting me.

I know that God has given us self-induced healing abilities and is a loving, creative, intelligent energy. I see this in the simplest things. I see it when a wound heals beneath a scab or bandage. Where does that wonderful ability come from? If that self-healing potential weren't there, each of us would bleed to death or die of infection from every cut or scratch.

When I see ice floating on a lake, I realize that water is the only liquid that when frozen becomes less dense. I think about why ice floats and realize what would happen to the life in that lake, and in our oceans, if water froze from the bottom up. I listen to a physicist discuss the expansion of the universe; he says that if the rate of expansion had been different by a trillion trillionth, the universe would not exist. And I begin to think, what or who is behind all this? I don't mean who in the sense of some wise old man or woman sitting up in Heaven, keeping track of everything, but this incredible awareness and intelligence that exists in life, in nature, in us. It is being a scientist that makes me spiritual. I can't accept all of this as coincidence.

I like to make a distinction between the words **religion** and **spiritual**. In our culture, for many of the people I see, religion can be a destructive force. In some cases religion seems to be teaching people that they deserve to suffer, they are sinners, and disease is an appropriate punishment. But I cannot accept this. Those are rules made by humans. If one accepts the messages of spirituality and love, grace is available to us all.

Religion can support you and in a sense hold you in the palm of its hand, or it can grasp and possess you. Too often, I think, we are possessed by religion. Spirituality is a healing force. With spirituality there are no rules related to God's love and God's ability to sustain us.

What Is the Meaning of Life?

When someone asks, "What do you think is the meaning of life?" I might answer: Life is an experience and an opportunity. The meaning comes from what we decide to do with the opportunity that is given to us.

I think we are, very simply, meant to love, and what we each need to do is to choose our way of loving the world. Then when you get up on Monday morning, you don't have to have your heart attack, because you're choosing your own path. You are looking forward to Monday morning and your way of contributing to the world.

To me the Garden of Eden represents the place where love **must** exist. But that would become boring—just picture us saying "I love you" to each other all day long. Once we are out of the Garden and into a place where love is a choice, then it really becomes meaningful. I think we are here to try to reflect back the love that created the universe, and to make this planet a place where children are loved and where pollution and self-destruction end because we love ourselves and therefore can spread that love. Alice Walker, the author, said, "We should always ask, 'Is it good for the children?'" I hope we can learn to see the world and one another in the way of the Native American Iroquois, who when they are making decisions think in terms of seven generations into the future. That vision should be incorporated into our lives too.

The purpose of our being here is to love. But it has to come freely, not as a burden. When we do this, we receive a gift. Karl Menninger said, "Love cures two people, the person who gives it and the person who receives it." We can understand that our differences are what make us beautiful, and that it is important that we have these differences.

Nature can be our teacher. I learn more by looking at nature than at anything else. And so when you have a problem I suggest that you go out and talk to a tree or a stream, or look at the ocean, and think, what would nature do if it had my problem? You will always get an answer. Nature knows how to deal with adversity, chaos and difficulties and how to continue, just as we do.

One day when I was out in the woods near our house walking our cat, Miracle (she thinks she is a dog, and I walk her on a leash), I found myself talking to a tree about a problem I was having. Then I walked around the tree and received my answer. Years earlier I had nailed part of a wire fence to that tree (the fence was to contain our son Jeff's goats and ornamental waterfowl). Now I noticed that the tree had grown around the fence. It had just incorporated the fence into its trunk. So the tree told me what to do: When something is irritating me, in my way I can grow around it and take it in.

Susan Duffy, the extraordinary woman I have mentioned to you, sent me a piece she wrote called "The Flower":

> Can you imagine a little seed being dropped by the winds in a cleft of a very high rock? It is a very beautiful flower as it grows into what it is supposed to be. Every day it greets the elements of life—the sun, the rain, the winds, and the darkness of night. It never complains or questions anything about its own existence. It just is. It is always completely obedient. Every day it is called to do and to be what it was made to be and to do. To open and shine, showing its face to God. In many cases a human eye will never see it, in its lifetime. There is only one that does see it, and that is God. It is in the silence of nature that one is open to all truth. Because only nature does what it is called upon to do in the perfect sense.

> The changing of the leaves in the fall is very symbolic to me. Just before the leaves drop from the trees they are at their most beautiful. Before you let go of the tree of life, you show your uniqueness and beauty. Green is a coverup. With these colorful leaves, God is reminding us of the importance of our differences.

Dr. Rachel Naomi Remen, a friend and physician, has experienced illness and surgery, so she is a native in both the world of the doctor and of the patient. In an article in the *Noetic Sciences Review* (Autumn, 1988) she says:

The purpose of life is to grow in wisdom and to learn to love better. If life serves these purposes, then health serves these purposes and illness serves them as well, because illness is part of life. . .

It is very interesting how often the process of physical healing runs concurrently with the healing of the heart. A greater altruism, a greater compassion, seems to occur in different people as you work with them through severe illness.

The Dalai Lama said, in the Spring 1990 issue of *Parabola* magazine:

The purpose of life is to serve other people. To do something of benefit for other people. From that point of view, a difficulty is really a great opportunity.

A friend of mine said, when his lover died of complications of AIDS:

The purpose of life is the growth of the soul. The body is not the measure of healing. Peace is the measure. And part of the healing is to accept and embrace death. People die when their work is done on the planet, or they die when they cease to grow. Many people do heal into death, resolving major life issues to completion. Healing does not necessarily mean you stay in the body. People with AIDS or life threatening diseases must come to terms with death. The more one resists or denies it, the more power it has. It is the quality of life that is the real issue.

If you ask, "I can choose to live or I can choose to die; I need something to live for—how do I find it?" I say, "Look around." If there is something else alive in your view when you raise your eyes, that is a reason to live. Fill your house with plants. Who's going to take care of them if you die? Get a pet. I know a woman who had a dozen cats. She couldn't die because she needed to take care of them.

Find someone who has more difficulties than you have. Look around you on the street: There are homeless people, drug addicts, young people who have lost their way. Get out there and do something for someone else who is in pain. Out of your pain you will find that you have a reason to live. The world is a difficult place. Run for the presidency, for that matter. Change the world. Society will not rescue you, but you may rescue society. Remember what it feels like to rescue a bird. If we all get our lives straightened out, the world is altered and healed.

I once called life a "beautiful burden," and someone got mad at me for calling it a burden. But I think it is like an enormous gift that is handed to you that may be hard to carry, and you may need some help carrying it.

Life is God's gift to us. What we do with it is our gift to God.

The Gift of Life

One of the questions I was shocked to hear people ask years ago was, "How do you know God doesn't want me to have cancer? Maybe God is punishing me with my disease." Today I am not surprised, because I understand better the source of the guilt and shame.

Disease isn't punishment; it is a part of life. If you are going to accept the gift of life, you're going to accept its difficulties. Natural disasters occur. (If you win the lottery, however, do you ask, "Why me?")

Everyone must die. And you are not a sinner if you have an affliction. It doesn't mean you didn't love enough or that you did something wrong; it simply is part of what life is about.

It is sad that people even consider such an idea, and it is a comment on how we are brought up. I see enormous conflict in the minds of some people as well as within a variety of religions. And some of it may stem from the religion itself. In 1829, Pope Leo XII declared that whoever allowed himself to be vaccinated ceased to be a child of God, that smallpox was a judgment of God and the vaccination a challenge toward Heaven.

Of course no one believes this any longer, but such beliefs can still have a subtle conscious and unconscious effect on people.

When Bobbie and I were visiting Ireland, several people in a cancer support group asked us if they should make an attempt to get better; they wondered if God wanted them to have cancer.

I believe we should understand that God didn't create the world to make people suffer. But I also believe that God knew we needed the freedom to experience all things in order to make life meaningful. I think the ideal approach to illness lies in the "Serenity Prayer," composed by Reinhold Niebuhr:

> God grant me serenity to accept the things I cannot change, courage to change the things I can, and wisdom to know the difference.

The Serenity Prayer includes all the things we're talking about: becoming a character and being uncooperative, as well as allowing and surrendering to the universe's schedule. We each have to decide what to fight for and what to allow. It is a personal choice.

If you consider Helen Keller, who became deaf and blind at nineteen months, you might think that here was somebody whose parents should have been devastated, who should have wondered, "What did we do wrong?" But if you read her words you will know that she never regarded her afflictions as a punishment; she confronted them as something to be overcome. I think that challenge came out of the fact that her parents were involved not in issues of guilt but with the question "What can we do for this child?"

Read what she says in her book *My Religion*:

> I have never believed that my limitations were in any sense punishments or accidents. If I had held such a view, I could never have exerted the strength to overcome them.

And:

> Difficulties meet us at every turn. They are the accompaniment of life. . . Out of pain grow the violets of patience and sweetness. . . The marvelous richness of human experience would lose something of rewarding joy if there were no limitations to overcome.

Using Every Resource: The Consultation

Faith in God can help us heal. Some people believe that this is enough, and they wonder, "Why do I need surgery?"

I think that God and our capabilities are quite powerful, but we are fallible. We can't always achieve everything we want to, and I believe in bringing in other resources. I mentioned the painting called "The

Consultation," in which doctor, patient, nurse, spiritual figure and medications are all present. I do know people who have said, "I left my troubles to God," and their cancer has gone away. If you think you're capable of doing that, fine.

But I also know that if you read the Bible, you learn that the physician is a resource, a gift from God. All medications stem from God. They're all, in a sense, natural. And so we can accept all things. Surgery and chemotherapy can be a gift from God. And when I see people doing drawings showing their treatment as a gift, or the operating room as a place where love and God exist, I know that they can incorporate their treatment into their lives. It becomes a part of God manifesting Himself, or Herself. (I often refer to God as female because I think our "female" qualities are related to healing and problem solving.)

All things become manifestations of God in a sense, including the surgeon and the therapy. They're all part of the same system, the same creation. And therefore all things by definition are God. One doesn't need to exclude anything. When you are capable of leaving your troubles to God, of getting on the universe's schedule, doing so makes everything simpler, including deciding the point at which you receive therapy.

I'm sure that someday we will find through research (some of which has already been done) that our consciousness can affect us and others, that our prayers affect others. That there is an energy available to all of us that can be used for healing. You can label this God if you want to, but we are God also. We are a part of this wonderful universal system. (When you get to Heaven you will be asked if you want to meet God, and if you say yes, you'll be asked how you want to be introduced. What will you answer? There is only one correct response. I hope you realize that you and God are one.)

While some people believe that everything should be left to God, others have asked, "Why does God have to play such a grand role in your philosophy? Don't you think that psychoneuroimmunology accounts for much of the explained so-called 'miracles'? Isn't all healing scientific?"

To me God **is** psychoneuroimmunology. My definition of God is intelligent, loving energy. God is scientific. God is light. God is darkness. God is all. (Please do not write to me to debate this. As Bobbie says, an atheist is a person with no invisible means of support. To help you understand this, when you get to Heaven, how will you describe yourself, your essence?)

Religion and science can come together. Certainly spirituality and science can come together. If you think of creativity and spirituality, think of things that Albert Einstein and other quantum physicists have said—they have seen the universe as incredible, awe-inspiring. They had a sense of the unity of the world and all the entities within it.

Making Choices

When I finish giving a lecture, people often come up afterward to ask questions, and some have even said, "I don't want to take up your time, so in the next thirty seconds please tell me what to do with my life." My response is, "How can you think so little of yourself that you ask me to decide what to do with your life, and especially in thirty seconds?" But they are frightened and insecure, and I think this question is really about making choices. The person may have to make a life choice now: where to live or what treatment to have.

What I have to think about is why others would want me to make that choice for them. One of the things I have noticed about exceptional patients is that they are not afraid to make choices. They realize that it is their life, and they take charge. They don't think,

"This is right if it cures me and if five years from now
I'm healthy." It is what is right now. They don't mind
redirecting their lives, changing their choices. But
when you are afraid to find your path, then you run to
me and say, "Can you light my way, please?" And if I
make a choice and you don't like it later, I'll be the vil-
lain.

Don't think so little of yourself that you allow other
people to make choices for you. Do they know your
story when they are about to make that decision? The
answer is no.

I can appreciate that what people are really asking
for is hope. That I can give them. It is easier to feel
comfortable and honest about giving hope than it is to
be making choices about someone else's life. We are all
unique, and no one knows the future for another individual. And so if people are willing to take on the challenge and do the fighting, I'm there to be with them.

An article appeared in the *Hartford Courant* (May
14, 1990) by Colin McEnroe about a woman named
Deborah Burton, who was pregnant and who also
learned she had cancer. She had many choices; including doing nothing about the cancer and having the
baby, having an abortion or having low-dose chemotherapy and continuing the pregnancy. These choices
would not be easily made, and they involved grave possible losses. She said that these words came to her:
"Embrace life." These were spoken, she said, almost
like a prayer. She went on:

> I knew what my heart wanted—but embracing
> that—feeling that my heart and I were okay, was
> the hard part. . .
>   I have this feeling about "wrong" decisions:
> that people make them at levels lower than where
> they're really at, and then they just resound into the
> future. I wanted to make mine at the highest level
> possible.

And I'd say those are key words. To make all decisions at the highest level possible. To affirm life—yours and that of others—and to move on.

Is Life Fair?

I sometimes ask people—at Wellness Society meetings, at psychological and medical meetings—if they think life is fair, and the majority always answer no. When I speak to fourth-year medical students at graduation, I try to get them to think by saying to them, "If life isn't fair, then don't go out and help people to live longer. Help them to die faster, so they don't have to put up with the unfairness." Many of them leave with a puzzled look, because I am making them think about what their role is.

But my feeling is that life is absolutely fair. It's just that we need to redefine the rules. Difficulties, problems, pain and losses come with life. And so our question becomes, how do we deal with those things? Can we use them as redirections and even look at them as gifts?

Katherine Mansfield in one of her letters said, "We have to find the gift in suffering." That "we can't afford to waste such an expenditure of feeling, we have to learn from it."

I learned many years ago that the genuinely happy people I meet are not happy because they have had only good fortune. I know that they are choosing their attitude.

At the hospital I used to give out pins to all the people who worked there I saw bringing love and happiness to those around them. I would walk up to them and say, "I'd like to know your name." I'm sure most of them thought, "Well, this is a doctor. He wants my name because I'm doing something wrong, and he'll report me." So they would just say their name. Then a month later I would bring them a pin with a rainbow on it, and their name, and give it to them as a gift. (Eventually in that way we created a subversive organization of lovers in the hospital.)

One day I went up to a medical secretary who was always surrounded by happy people. I said, "I'd like to know your name."

She said, "Why?" I said, "Because I want to give you a gift. You create this aura of happiness around you, and I want to thank you for it." And she replied, "Sit down, I have a story to tell you. I've been here two years," she said. "When I took the job I signed a contract, came to work, and was immediately surrounded by miserable people. I mean the doctors and nurses—the patients weren't a problem. So I went down to the office at lunchtime and said, 'I refuse this job. I quit.' And they said, 'You can't quit; you have to give two weeks' notice.' I said, 'All right, I'll give you two weeks' notice then.' I got up every day unhappy, until the last day of the two weeks, and then I got up so happy that it was my last day, that I went to work happy. And I realized something at the end of the day. All the people around me were happy. So I didn't quit, I just decided to come in happy."

And that is a choice each of us is capable of making. We must realize that the joy and light are created within us; they don't come from outside.

In a way, the course of life itself is unfair for all of us. One solution to this that I have been thinking about would be to live life backward. We could die first and get that out of the way, and then we would grow younger. I came across a wonderful poem suggesting this. It appeared in the newsletter for the Life Center of Indianapolis, contributed by Norm Glass:

Life is tough.
It takes up a lot of your time,
all your weekends,
and what do you get at the end of it?
. . . Death, a great reward.
I think that the life cycle is all backwards.
You should die first, get it out of the way.
Then you live twenty years in an old age home.
You get kicked out when you're too young,
you get a gold watch, you go to work.
You work forty years until you're
young enough to enjoy your retirement.
You go to college,
you party until you're ready for high school,
you become a little kid, you play,
you have no responsibilities,
you become a little boy or girl,
you go back into the womb,
you spend your last nine months floating.
And you finish off as a gleam in someone's eye.

I like to say jokingly at workshops that I have
served as an outside advisor on the Board of Directors
of Heaven—that each year God selects three men and
three women to help Her keep up to date on current
topics. And that God gives each of us at the end of our
term a plaque that reads: "Don't feel totally, personally,
irrevocably, eternally responsible for everything. That's
my job," and the plaque is signed "God." I think that
message ought to make us all feel better and lighten
our burdens.

There Are No Unforgivable Sins

I described in my book *Peace, Love & Healing* that I
once had a dream in which I was told to read Samuel

Taylor Coleridge's "The Ancient Mariner." When I went to the bookstore to find it, there lying on the counter was a beautiful illustrated copy. I don't think that was a coincidence. I picked up the book and looked at it, wondering what I needed to know. And these lines toward the end leaped out at me:

> He prayeth well, who loveth well
> Both man and bird and beast.
> He prayeth best, who loveth best
> All things both great and small;
> For the dear God who loveth us,
> He made and loveth all.

I realized, first, that this was telling me that there are no exceptions to God's love and that there shouldn't be to our love for each other. There are no exceptions to the rule of love and forgiveness—if we are going to choose love, we must love everyone.

Another part of the poem also struck me. The Ancient Mariner is sitting with the dead albatross tied around his neck:

> The selfsame moment I could pray;
> And from my neck so free
> The Albatross fell off, and sank
> Like lead into the sea.

When I read those lines I knew that through everything that happens to us, there is a resource available. God resides in each of us.

In this connection I want to make a point related to misunderstanding or criticism of something I said in the past.

Emmet Fox in talking about love said that there is no disease that enough love will not overcome. We could be very critical, then, of some people and say they didn't love enough. But the point he and I are trying to make is that in a sense the fundamental disease that we all suffer from is not loving yourself enough. And that may come from having not been loved, and then being incapable of loving others. That's a disease.

I meet people with a variety of life-threatening illnesses, with the inability of many parts of their bodies to function, and yet they are living a life of love and are incredible inspirations and examples to others. That is the point I am trying to make. Not that you haven't loved enough, but that your body doesn't limit your ability to love, and that when you are confronting life-threatening problems, or are quadriplegic, or have had arms and legs blown off by hand grenades, you can still be a lover, and still function. The essence of this truth is contained in a quotation in Dr. Richard Selzer's book *Down from Troy: A Doctor Comes of Age.* His father, a general practitioner, said, "True good health is the ability to do without it."

In *Peace, Love & Healing,* I also mentioned a clergyman who in a sermon talked about Jeremiah's viewing the potter and how he reworked the clay. The minister concluded the sermon by saying, "There is only one unforgivable sin, backing away from life when you've made a mess of things." The message was that we shouldn't quit—we should rework things, we should redo things, we should never give up on life.

Several people wrote to me about that line to say, "There are no unforgivable sins." And I do agree. What you do isn't unforgivable. God isn't the problem. If you asked, "God, can you forgive me?" the answer would be "Yes, that's my job." But you must forgive yourself and others and seek their forgiveness. God is not the problem.

This is stated in the Koran too, wherein God says:

Oh my servants, who have been too harsh with your souls, with yourselves, despair not the mercy of God, for God forgives all sins.

I think that God is far more liberal than people are. If an individual is willing to learn from what he or she has done, then who are we humans to withhold forgiveness? It is our problems and our bitterness that make us hold grudges.

The only thing that is going to save people and save the world is if we forgive and love each other. And then healing can come. It doesn't mean that I have to like everything that you have done. But not to forgive means that there are things that I can't forgive myself for either. Everything is forgivable once one understands why people are the way they are.

In the Bible we are told that Jesus said to a man who was paralyzed, "Your sins are forgiven." Jesus knew that the important point was to heal your life, because a life can be healed, even without a cured disease. Someone with cerebral palsy or paraplegia or cancer or AIDS can still exist in the context of a healed life.

The author Joseph Heller wrote a book (with his friend Speed Vogel) called *No Laughing Matter*, about his experience with paralysis due to a disease of the nervous system. He told about the visits of many of his friends, including Mel Brooks, who came into his room and said, "For Jesus! Stand! Walk!" Heller tried his best, but failed. Mel Brooks said, "I thought I'd give it a shot." I wrote to Mel Brooks and told him to say "your sins are forgiven," next time he wants to help a friend.

I know how much we need forgiveness for our acts in order to begin to live or die peacefully. I have literally walked through a nursing home saying, "Your sins are forgiven," and people get very quiet when they hear this.

Edward Salisbury, who has had some near-death experiences, has devoted his life to care of the aging and ill; he wrote to me after I had talked about how healing this statement is. He told me that in the early

1980s, he worked the 3 P.M. to 11 P.M. shift as a nurse's aide in a nursing home, giving "primary care" to residents who seemed to be waiting to die. It was his habit to say goodnight to some of the patients who insisted that he not leave before doing so.

One woman, "Mrs. D.," became very close to him and often questioned him about his belief in forgiveness. She had been unable to walk for more than six years, and he would transfer her from her wheelchair to her commode or bed. She waited every night for him to tuck her in and kiss her goodnight before she would go to sleep. They had many long talks about God, death and family.

> One evening as I headed out the door toward my car feeling exhausted and grateful that the evening's work was over, I heard a high-pitched, mournful cry from the window overlooking the parking lot. It stopped me in my tracks. I realized I had failed to say goodnight to Mrs. D.

He returned to her room and found her sitting upright in her bed looking anguished and upset. She scolded him, then asked him to sit with her a bit.

> As we talked, I realized that she wanted to discuss matters of great importance to her. She asked, "Do you think God will forgive everything?" I had spoken to her and others of my near death experiences and my absolute knowing that God is all loving and all forgiving. I recognized that she was holding a great sense of shame and guilt. So I reassured her that there was nothing she could have done that would prevent her from receiving God's Love and Grace.
> She told me, "When I was a young woman I stole my parents' fine silver so my fiancé and I could elope. I never talked to them again. I feel so

bad and ashamed. I've never told this to anyone and I am afraid God will not forgive me."

I leaned close to her and said, "I know that God forgives you. God knows you and only wants you to **know** his **love**."

He put her to bed and left. The next morning when he came in, the administrator and the nursing director were waiting for him. They asked, "What did you say to Mrs. D. last night?" He replied that they had talked about love and forgiveness. They said:

> Last night at about 2 A.M. Mrs. D. **walked** all the way down the hall from her room to the nurses' station, put her Bible and her teeth on the counter and said, "I won't be needing these anymore, thank you." She walked unassisted back to her bed, lay down and died.

She died with peace of mind. Obviously the forgiveness helped heal her life. I hope we will all be able to forgive ourselves, because God certainly has forgiven us. I mean forgive ourselves so that we can live fully, accepting every part of ourselves—not just be forgiven so we can end our lives, but so that we can begin them.

Accepting Your "Shadow"

According to Carl Jung, the "shadow" stands for the dark, unexplored part of ourselves—the part we often project onto someone or something else if we don't explore and accept it. He illustrated this in a colorful way: "If God is at the front door, the Devil will be at the back door." I understand that within me lies a potential murderer—and once I know that, I don't become a murderer; I can deal with that part of myself. Accepting my own shadow makes it easier to accept someone else's.

We have to understand that there is a big difference between loving and liking. I'm not asking people to like what a criminal has done. But if you know that you yourself could be a criminal, it will be easier to understand the criminal, and love can lead to rehabilitation and healing, not just punishment and incarceration.

Let me quote again from one of my favorite books, William Saroyan's *The Human Comedy* (I hope that if you haven't read it, you will):

> The evil do not know they are evil and are therefore innocent, the evil man must be forgiven every day. He must be loved because something of each of us is in the most evil man in the world, and something of him is in each of us. He is ours and we are his. None of us is separate from any other. The peasant's prayer is my prayer, the assassin's crime is my crime.

Two Tales About Tigers

I like to tell a story in workshops that is true in spirit, anyhow, about my experience with a tiger. I think it says a lot about the meaning of life:

Bobbie and I were going to speak one night in one of the major cities in the United States. We had the afternoon free and so we went to the zoo. As we were walking along the path enjoying all the animals out in their natural environments (they were fenced in rather than caged), I was commenting to Bobbie on how wonderful and real all this looked. Suddenly, we saw a tiger in front of us. I said, "Look, see how beautiful that is? You can get up close and look."

Then we got a little closer and realized that there was no fence between the tiger and us. So I sent Bobbie for help while I stood still, hoping the tiger would just look at me and that nothing would happen. Bobbie could run back up the path and get help. But the tiger seemed to be taking an interest in me. So I climbed over a very steep vertical ledge and hung on to a vine that was there, knowing that the tiger couldn't reach me. The tiger just sat down, put its head on it paws— just like our cat at home—and watched me. I felt safe.

After a while I thought I might as well climb down and get away. But as I started to climb down, I heard a roar. I looked up and saw that the tiger hadn't moved, but as I looked down I saw that another tiger had appeared and was roaring up at me. So I just hung on to the vine, knowing that my wife would eventually show up. And as I was hanging there, feeling safe, I felt some powder on my head. I looked up and there was a white mouse eating away at the vine. But since it was a big, thick vine, I knew that I had plenty of time.

A little while later I looked up again, feeling more powder falling, and there was a black mouse eating toward the white mouse. I was getting a little bit nervous. And when I get nervous, I get hungry. Hanging on the vine was a bunch of grapes, so I grabbed them and ate them, and they were the sweetest, most delicious grapes that I'd ever had in my life. And my reaction was to say, "Ah!"

And that really what life is about. The tiger of your birth is up above, the tomb of the womb. Down below is the tiger of your death, the womb of the tomb. Day and night are eating away at you. So your job is to live now, in this moment.

Experience life and say—"Ah!"

Joseph Campbell tells a story at the end of the book *The Hero's Journey* about an orphaned little tiger that was brought up by goats. He didn't know he was a

tiger, and he bleated and ate grass along with the goats.
Then one day a male tiger pounced on the little flock,
and they scattered.

> But this little fellow was a tiger, he wasn't a goat.
> So there he was, standing. The big fellow looked at
> him. And he said, "What, **you** living here with
> these goats?" The little tiger goes **Maaaaaa** and
> begins nibbling grass in a kind of embarrassed way.

> The big fellow took him by the neck, carried him to
> a pond, and said,

> "Now look into that pond." And the little one puts
> his face over it. And for the first time in his little
> life he sees his actual face.

When the pond is still we become aware of our eternal
presence not being someone else. The ripples confuse
our identity—here I come, there I go. Anyhow, the little
tiger's beginning to sort of get the message. The big fellow's next discipline is to pick him up and take him to his
den, where there are the remains of a recently slaugh-
tered gazelle. The big fellow takes a chunk of this bloody
stuff, and he says to the little one, "Open your face."

The little one backs off. He says, "I'm a vegetarian."

"Well," says the big one, "none of that nonsense."
And he shoves it down his throat. And the little one
gags on it, as the text says, "As all do on true doctrine."

So, gagging on the true doctrine, it's nevertheless
getting into his system since it is his proper food, and it
activates his proper nervous system. Spontaneously
moved by his proper food, he gives a little tiger roar,
sort of Tiger Roar 101. Then the big guy says, "There
we are. Now we've got it. Now we'll eat tiger food."

There's a moral here, of course. It is that we're all
really tigers living here as goats. The function of sociol-

ogy and most of our religious education is to teach us to be goats. But the function of the proper interpretation of mythological symbols and meditation discipline is to introduce you to your tiger face. Then comes the problem. You've found your tiger face but you're still living here with these goats. How are you going to do that?

What you will have learned is through all the forms of the world, the one radiance of eternity shows itself. You can regard the appearance of the miracle of life in all these forms. But don't let them know that you are a tiger! . . . You wear the outer garment of the law; you behave like everyone else. And you wear the inner garment of the mystic way. Now that's the great secret of life.

This is what we are talking about—finding your way of loving the world, not ignoring the world, or truly being indifferent. Parents, teachers, religious leaders—these authority figures can turn us into goats when we're born little tigers. The key is to find the tiger in yourself.

Where people gag on true doctrine, please remember that when you are trying to change people, you are better off telling stories, anecdotes. If you come dressed as a goat, people won't know that there is the inner role of the mystic and the tiger in you. When you dress like a goat they are more likely to listen to your tigertalk.

I arrived at one workshop driving a 1969 Chevrolet Camaro that was basically rusting away; it was at our house to be restored by our son Stephen. The whole day people listened to me intently, and at the end of the day a woman came up to me and said, "You have had a profound effect on us, because of your humble nature." I said, "How do you know anything about my humble nature?" She said, "Oh, we saw the car you're driving. If you had come in a Mercedes, you couldn't have affected us in this way." And so, you will understand what I mean when I say, "Come as a goat."

8
The Bridge: Letting Go and Finding Peace

I was a labor nurse for nine years prior to my entrance into hospice nursing. So many similarities are present at birth and death. If as a patient is dying I can help them or their families recall birth and the hard work involved in this natural life process, somehow death is much less mysterious and frightening. I want to teach people to be present with these loved ones at this most incredible time. . . I am in the process of teaching seminars called "Midwifing to the Dying," and how to witness, validate and be present at this life event.

—JAN BERNARD

Touching the Edge of Death

People sometimes ask how they can "face the death issue." I think this means accepting the fact that we are mortal. We all have a limited amount of time here, whether it is one day, or twenty or sixty years. Live the day or the years—that is the key.

One woman said, "I have cancer, but I am still a young person with children to raise. I don't feel ready to face death at all."

You have children to raise. What is it that you want your children to know? If you weren't here, what would they have? They would have the memory of your voice, telling them that you love and accept them no matter what. But maybe you also want to give them letters, or even a videotape of yourself just reminding them that you love them and that when difficulties come, God is redirecting them. So they can grow up with messages from you that are going to stay with them no matter what happens to you. Show them how to deal with adversity and afflictions. What would you want to leave behind, what would you want to share with them, what would you want to teach them? I think if they know they are loved, and that difficulties lie ahead but that life is about what we can contribute, they will make it through.

I suggest to you and to everyone: Make a will. Do it and get it off your mind. Are there treasures you want people to have? Write out anything that you feel people need to know. And it's quite possible that when you do all the things you want to do before you die, you may feel too good to die. One way I evaluate hospices is to ask if they have graduation ceremonies. Because people can heal their lives in preparation for dying, and then feel better and so get sent home.

Start now to do some of the things you have always wanted to do. If you have always wished for a dog or a cat, if you have wanted to plant a garden, study a language, or go camping with your children—whatever it is, do it, so that you are living to the fullest now. Live in short time segments to make them meaningful.

I think that is the way to face the death issue. Not that you become depressed about the fact that you could die of cancer or AIDS or heart disease, but that you accept the fact that death is an event we all must confront.

Denying it will not help. What do you have to do to get ready? What do you need to do to complete your life?

Sadness and grief I can understand, because of separation from your family. But then I would ask, what is there about death that frightens you? What are the things you need to confront? Talk about your fears so that you are in charge of your death and maybe even the details of your funeral. What music do you want to have played? What do you want it to be like? This may seem morbid, but I'd rather deal with those issues and not make them significant events that wear me out.

At one of our workshops in Chicago, a beautiful

lady in her eighties said that when she learned she had cancer, she called her children and her husband together, and they discussed her funeral—the music, the caterer, all of the details. The children were upset by the conversation, but she sat them down and they went through the plans together. And, of course, she didn't die. But all the plans have been made.

When my father and his brother were younger and were helping care for the family cemetery plot, they would actually lie down on the places that were their future burial sites and decide which exposure they wanted, which one would give them the most sun.

Why is that meaningful? Because they were confronting their mortality. But the beautiful and even humorous thing was that when it came time to put my father's coffin into the ground, the men doing it picked up the coffin, turned it around and placed it in just the position my dad had decided on. That brought a smile to our lips. He lived fully until he died and then made sure we followed his instructions.

I'd ask you to do that, so that your children don't grow up afraid of the same things that you are afraid of but are stronger individuals because of you.

There is a special person whose words I want to share with you. He had been a wonderful athlete, but then he was diagnosed with cancer. He had central nervous system involvement and tumors in the brain and lung. He went through operations, chemotherapy and radiation, experiencing many side effects and even going into a coma. But he never lost his spirit, and he recovered to participate in swimming, skiing and other athletic events. Later he had a series of strokes but recovered again, even though he had lost his sight. He believed that, even in a coma, one's spirit can begin the journey to another plane. He came close to death many times, and saw the white light, experienced the peaceful miracle, a powerful yet gentle spirit who some day will lead us through transition and deliver us from despair. And I believe we can take with us the greatest treasure we can accumulate in this life, love and hope. There is indeed a bridge between the two worlds.

He reminds me of a patient who left a note for me before she died, saying, "Thanks for all the love. I can take it with me."

I have described how many years ago I had a dream, and in the dream I was told to read the book *Journey to Ixtlan* by Carlos Castenada. When I went to the bookstore and got the book, I found that there was much in it that I needed to learn. It always amazes me how the unconscious seems to be aware of what we need to know and to lead us to it.

One of the sections of *Journey to Ixtlan* that I felt was meant for me concerned death. In it, Carlos is being taught by Don Juan, and after Carlos says he thinks it would be meaningless to dwell upon death, since such a thought would only bring discomfort and fear, Don Juan responds:

> You're full of crap. Death is the only wise advisor that we have. Whenever you feel, as you always do, that everything is going wrong and you're about to be annihilated, turn to your death and ask it if that is so. Your death will tell you that you're wrong and nothing really matters outside its touch. Your death will tell you "I haven't touched you yet." Look at me, I have no doubts or remorse. Everything I do is my decision and my responsibility. The simplest thing I do—to take you for a walk in the desert, for instance—may very well mean my

death. Death is stalking me. Therefore I have no room for doubts or remorse. If I have to die as a result of taking you for a walk, then I must die. You, on the other hand, feel that you are immortal and the decisions of an immortal man can be canceled or regretted or doubted. In a world where death is the hunter, my friend, there is not time for regrets or doubts, there is only time for decisions.

Carlos asks a little later: "Is it so terrible to be a timid man?"

Don Juan responds:

No, it isn't if you are going to be immortal, but if you are going to die, there is no time for timidity. Simply because timidity makes you cling to something that exists only in your thoughts. It soothes you while everything is at a lull, but then the awesome mysterious world will open its mouth for you, as it will open for every one of us and then you will realize that your sure ways were not sure at all. Being timid prevents us from examining and exploiting our lot as men.

Enjoy yourself. It is later than you think.

Death Is Not Failure

A chaplain asked, "I am uncomfortable when the term 'failing' is applied to patients who are approaching death. I believe death is one of God's and nature's forms of healing (not 'failure')! Any suggestion for an alternative term?"

I agree with him that we need to deal with this issue. It isn't that we need to come up with another term. We have a term. It's called dying. Somebody died. Let's talk about it. Not "they bought the farm" or "kicked the bucket" or "passed away." Let's talk about it so that we confront these things.

I taught a college course in which the textbook had two or three pages of ways to say someone died without using the word **dead**. And these terms are used in hospitals; I hear them all the time. At Yale, the staff (I don't) talks about patients "Bradying" because the morgue is in the Brady Building. When a friend of mine died in the intensive-care unit and I asked the next morning what had happened to him, the secretary said, "He Bradied." I could not get her to say that he had died.

But we can see death as a form of healing. Let us say to one another, "If you're tired and need to go, it's okay." My mother gave my father permission to go, to leave his body. We had gotten a hospital bed for him, to have in the house, and one day my mother called to tell me, "Dad is saying, 'I need to get out of here, Rose.'" She interpreted that to mean he didn't like the hospital bed, but I said, "Mom, it's his body he needs to get out of, not the bed." And she understood. He didn't fail us; he left, surrounded by his loved ones at three o'clock in the afternoon. And every single person whom he loved who could get there was there. He waited for all of us. He took his last breath and left when the last person walked into the room. And something beautiful was accomplished.

We'll discuss more at the conclusion of this book about how he could die with a smile on his face, and what we shared in those last moments. If we can understand that death isn't a failure, then we'll feel comfortable in using the word **dying**.

I may add that when some people are granted permission to go, they recover or as one woman put it "I'm not going anywhere." Their spirit plays a part in their will to live. I've seen this happen in intensive care units and the operating room.

I see this in the drawings people make. When the spiritual color purple is used, such as with a purple balloon or kite that is moving out of the picture, I interpret this as the artist's saying, "I'm ready to leave." To me the person is saying, "My body is not a place I want to be anymore." It doesn't mean you wouldn't like to live a hundred years if you were well. But you say, "I'm ready to go, so let me go." And then leaving the body is a spiritual transition and is your next form of healing. You're whole again.

I'll always remember a lady who had had an arm amputated as treatment for cancer forty years earlier. But now she drew a picture of herself with two arms. Now if you haven't had an arm for forty years, how do you put it back on again? Well, the drawing told me that she was ready to die and that she was feeling totally whole again. When you die, in a sense all the parts are back.

These people haven't failed. They have become healed.

I received a letter from a woman saying:

I have lived and loved every day, and the life I have right at this moment is a gift. . . . I am not a disease or the ugliness of the disease. I know that my spirit and light heal, and radiate a light that is beyond all knowing and beauty, and it is that beauty I am. It is my spirit that will live for all time, and it is that enduring part of me that I carry to eternity and will celebrate in the presence of my God. I wouldn't have missed it for the world.

A young man who was a medical student and who was suffering from cancer wrote wonderful letters to his friends (his parents, Sue and Bob Clark, shared these with me after his death). In one of these he wrote:

> Your support keeps my spirits up. Thank you. I feel that I must tell you that even if I do not achieve my dreams in the form that I dream them, I know that it is not because God has failed me, it is not because my family failed me, it is not because my friends failed me, it is not because my doctors failed me, and it is not because I failed me. It may be that my body failed me.

His mother said, "He lived all of his life. He died hugging a nurse and lived all of the way. We are so proud of him."

At a workshop a participant asked, "I'm not so much afraid of dying as of dying by inches. How does one get control and stay in control and get rid of the fears?"

My answer is that instead of thinking in terms of "control," think about peace of mind. When we try to be in control, that's when the artificiality comes—when people are hurting but smile anyway, saying, "I'm okay, nobody will know I'm out of control." One man used to say, "My disease is an inconvenience." He put on such a performance it was killing him. None of his neighbors knew how sick he was. He would collapse every time he walked into his living room and then have to be carried to bed. But he'd stay there all night, pull himself together and get out the next morning. He wasn't in control; he was just denying and performing.

If you want to be in control, confront your fears, like the fear of "dying by inches." What does this mean? Perhaps we die in a sense by inches when we have conflicts. Resolve the conflicts. Dying by inches may get you to understand your value and worth. How many inches still make life worth living? Do you die if you can't work, or walk? Is life worthwhile if you can see your family and be loved one hour a day? These are questions you are capable of answering, and you can decide if there aren't enough inches or minutes left to appreciate life. Understand that if you're ready to die, it's okay. If that is your choice and you are ready to leave your body, you can die at home, surrounded by loved ones, and not fail anyone.

Marilynn Rivest, a young lady who had breast cancer and was a social worker, came to our ECaP groups; she had sponsored several talks that I gave. She told me that she was going to Florida to die among her friends. When she got there, one of her friends was working with autistic children and dolphins, and he got her into the water with the dolphins. Their love and affection and gentleness changed her and prolonged her life. She felt beauty and peace in the relationship with them; she learned so much from them. Several years later, when she was tired and ready to go, she came home to Connecticut. She called me one night and said she was having trouble dying. And I said, "That's funny, I've never had a phone call from a dolphin." The next morning her parents called and thanked me, because she had died quietly and peacefully that night.

So be a dolphin, if you will. Get back to your instincts, to the part of you that knows how to live and how to die. Don't let society take over. Don't let others tell you what is right or wrong for you. Live your life and you won't die by inches. When you get ready to die, you will die.

I see that in our ECaP groups; more than ninety percent of the people in the groups who have died have never needed a hospice facility. Why not? Well, what is a hospice for? To resolve life situations and difficulties, to deal with physical and emotional problems and help you in your dying process—a very worthy and important role. But if you've lived fully, dying isn't a problem. And so our group members who have lived fully have shared all of that, and when they get ready to die, they die. Now it may be a day, it may be a week later, because they may be waiting for somebody to come and visit. But it isn't a process of inches, it's one of completion.

Another woman asked, "How does one embrace death in a positive way when it seems the ultimate loss of control?"

Death isn't "loss of control" by my definition. We are living with the gift of life, a gift we are trying to use to its greatest potential. We're not ever in control of anything. This doesn't mean that we are not responsible and that we don't live fully. But being in control is an illusion. Only our thoughts are ours to control. Our choices are ours. As the nurse who worked in labor delivery and hospice said, death is a transition, like birth.

Some of us are trying to avoid change. But change is inevitable. Aging is inevitable. I'd say to confront it and use it. If you get back to living in the moment, what age are you? You're ageless. You are enjoying the moment. Most of us won't accept that.

Now I know that as I get older, I can't run as fast or as far as I did years ago. But I can still participate and enjoy an activity as if I were still a child. So in a sense, the peace that comes with the activity, with the meaningfulness of the day, stops you from focusing on death. If you ask me what is the best day of my life?, I'd answer, today.

I have run three marathons in my life and trained for four. The second time I overtrained and hurt myself, and I couldn't participate. But in 1991, the third time I ran, I trained more sensibly. I ran with our daughter-in-law, Judy, who is a young physician, and our son Jonathan, an attorney. Judy knew that one of the reasons I was running again was to hear the woman who shouts, "You're all winners!" She was there again that year. Judy heard her too, and that helped make my day.

I have said that God gives us signs when we are on the right path. William Saroyan's *The Human Comedy* includes a scene in which two brothers are walking down the street. One tugs the other and points, and there is a Lincoln penny, face up.

> "A penny," Homer said. "Pick it up, Ulysses, it's good luck. Keep it always." And Ulysses picked up the penny. And looked around at everybody smiling at his good luck.

When I was about to begin the first marathon, with twenty-six miles lying ahead of me, I felt I needed a sign that I was on the right path, and I found a quarter beneath my feet on the starting line, and a penny many miles later. So this time I looked again, and wondered if I would find my twenty-six cents. (I share my craziness with people. I'm not afraid to.) Lo and behold, in the grass, standing with 25,000 people before the race started, I found a penny. I thought there was very little chance of finding a quarter in the streets of New York, but many miles later, lying there in front of us as we ran the marathon course, was a quarter. I like to think of this, too, as a sign that I was on my path, and that God was having a little fun with me.

I'm proud to say that 21,000 people finished the race before I did. I'm proud because I realize it was the participating, the joy of the three of us coming to the finish line together, that meant the most. Fred Lebow, the organizer of the race, said that he admires most the people who take five hours to finish, because for them it is so much harder. Everyone got a medal, and I'm proud of mine.

The fourth time, I ran to celebrate my sixtieth birthday. Fred Lebow, who had had brain cancer three years before, also ran and motivated people to run to raise money for cancer care and research. The passion comes on us when we are afflicted. Fred Lebow received more than 2,000 letters congratulating him for running after having treatment for cancer.

That time I ran alone, to be with myself. Jon and Judy finished before I did. I finished number 22,530, but only 545 people my age ran. In my age group I was right in the middle.

Once again I learned that we are all winners.

What I know about embracing death is that my own time will come. It will be sad for me to say good-bye to my family, to life, to the flowers. As I look around me right now, I am surrounded by beauty, by the sky and creation. I don't want to leave, but if at some point I cannot be a part of this beauty, if my body isn't functioning any more, if I am the flower or the leaf that's ready to fall, it will be time.

And so I will embrace the next step, the next healing, which will be to go. I think there is more to us, and that we do exist in some other form when the body ends. I think it is damned exciting that we move on and go ahead to a new adventure. So I embrace the adventure of death, as well as feel saddened by it, and I hope that I can do it in as beautiful a manner as some of my loved ones and group members have done it.

I want to be able to take it as a challenge. When I train and run a marathon, I confront myself and my body. I want to see death in the same way, to confront and face it. By the time I die I hope I have stopped being afraid of everything, including death. If I have achieved that, then I will be ready. If there are things I haven't completed, yes, I'll be upset. Maybe a painting I want to do, someone I want to talk to—it's possible I can run out of time. Knowing me, I probably will. But I'm going to work like hell to get it all in, so that when death comes knocking I can say, "Hello, friend. I'm sore. Take me in your arms, embrace me. I am ready to go with you."

The surprising thing for me is that when I taught a class at a local college—Southern Connecticut State University—during the first session I asked all the students to fill out their death certificates. It was incredible to see how these young people were writing on their death certificates that they were going to die in their thirties, or forties or fifties, of all kinds of tragic events. I had on my own death certificate that I would die at ninety-eight. I would be climbing a ladder to do some work on the roof of the house, and the family would all be there because it was my birthday; they would be yelling at me that I shouldn't be up there doing what I was doing at my age. And I would fall from the ladder and die.

Recently I had reason to think back to what I had written on my death certificate for that class. I think I know myself too well, and I'd better learn to change some of my habits.

On the Fourth of July we had had a picnic at our son Jeffrey's house, and when we returned home Bobbie went in to take a nap. I set up our old wooden ladder against the house; it looked in fine condition. I climbed up on the roof to cut off a limb; I was carrying an extension saw in my hand. As I got back onto the ladder and took the first step, the rung snapped. Apparently part of it had rotted, and putting my support on that end snapped it, and I fell fourteen or sixteen feet. I don't remember the fall, I can tell you that my life didn't flash in front of me, and it wasn't spiritual, I just said, "Oh, God." And down I went. I must have managed to hold on to the ladder so my feet and back hit first, and the next thing I remember was my head hitting the blacktop in our driveway. I was pretty woozy for several minutes and just lay there. I sustained a mild concussion. But the thing that I realized again was of course that life is very uncertain. Had one of my feet gotten caught in the rung and had I gone down head first instead of onto my feet, I might not be here writing this book. So I think we all need to learn that life is uncertain, and to live it fully.

I remember, too, a different experience with the closeness of death. When I was four years old, I was sitting on my bed, home sick with an ear infection. I had taken apart a toy telephone. Obviously it wasn't a very safe toy. I put the parts in my mouth because I knew carpenters and workmen did those things. The big men. That's how they worked. So I filled my mouth with parts of the toy and aspirated them and was choking to death. I felt totally peaceful, and I can still recall that feeling as I was sitting there. I knew that dying was not a problem. Even as a four-year-old, I had a very spiritual sense of that moment. But I was upset because I knew that my mother—whom I could see in the kitchen but couldn't call out to—would come in, see me dead and say, "What a terrible child, he died." That's how I felt, as if I were being a very bad boy by dying. A good child didn't do that. (Isn't guilt wonderful?)

And then suddenly I vomited, and all those parts came flying out, and I could breathe again. I also had a sense that someone had made a decision that I wasn't to die at that moment—perhaps the same energy, or force or God, that saved me when I fell off the ladder.

In any case I can tell you that our son Jeffrey has bought me a new ladder—much better made. It can't rust, rot or conduct electricity. I'm sure that it will outlast me.

Dying on Schedule

There are all kinds of signs—in dreams, poems and drawings—that people have precognitions of death. I remember a poem that appeared in our local newspaper; it had been written by one of the people who died when a commercial jet lost a cargo door. The poem, which was written weeks before the flight, was about being sucked out into a vacuum and sinking into the sea. When you read this you say, "Wow, he knew."

Accidents happen, but sometimes we choose when we die. We see this when we look at an article called "Postponement of Death until Symbolically Meaningful Occasions" which appeared in the *Journal of the American Medical Association*. The statistics revealed that, in every culture, more people die after birthdays and holidays. When we have something to look forward to, we can hang on. There is a will within us and a fight to be a part of meaningful events. I hear people say, "I'm going to die at two o'clock when the kids arrive from California," and this is indeed what happens.

People have had dreams about things like getting on an airplane or dying on a certain day or in an operating room. And these things have happened often enough so that I know we have an intuitive sense.

If you get messages of that sort, don't get on the plane. Don't have surgery on a certain day, if dying on the operating table on Thursday was something you dreamed. One lady dreamed that "Thursday" was printed on her headstone. We didn't operate on Thursday, and that made the two of us feel better.

I received a letter from a man who had written "Dying on Schedule" on the envelope. I don't know that anyone really dies based on an external schedule, but rather on their personal schedule of life.

A nurse wrote to me from France and told me about a thirty-year-old man with extensive cancer who wanted to see his daughter's First Holy Communion. The big day arrived, she said, and his daughter came to see him in her Communion dress. He looked completely happy, in spite of his condition, and "on the following day he died, having achieved his goal."

If you achieve your goal, then it's part of your schedule. It doesn't mean that we want to be dead, but there is a point at which leaving our bodies is the next form of therapy.

One woman, Patricia Zacharias, told me that her father had cancer, but no one would face this fact. After she read my books she brought everybody together, shared her love and let her father know that by dying he was not leaving them. They cried, hugged, kissed and loved for the remainder of his days. Her father felt at peace. He began having "out of body" experiences. She wrote:

> He prepared his living will and funeral arrangements. He even asked what he'd be wearing at the funeral. He suggested his green golf sport jacket and wanted us to make sure he was wearing his Nike sneakers because they were his best pals during his last months of ambulation. . . During his last week he felt that he was traveling through a long tunnel with a bright light at the end with beautiful colors. This was fascinating to me because my father was never one to express himself in those ways.

Another woman shared what her fourteen-year-old son, Thomas Connor, wrote a week before he died, as part of a school paper:

> Some people think that death is a great relief; they think of life as a punishment, and that death is a "better prison" at the end of all of life's

sorrows. . . But life has more highs than lows. . . In
the end you will welcome death, not as an escape
from life and all its hardships, but as a final reward
from all its highs and lows.

A week after Thomas Connor's death, a minister
spoke about him in his sermon. The minister hadn't
known her son, the boy's mother said, but "if he had,
he would have been aware that he always remembered
his thank-yous when he was halfway out the door." The
minister told his congregation:

> God gives each soul a new life. And God looked up
> and saw a soul in front of him and said, "It's a
> short life, only fourteen years, but they're good
> years." And the soul said, "That's all right. That's
> okay. I'll take it." And with a leap and a bound he
> was off, scampering down the hill towards the
> gates. And as quickly as he started, he slid to a stop
> and turned back to God, whose eyes had never left
> him. "And thank you," he shouted. "Thank you."

A woman said of her father:

> His disease kept progressing, but I felt he
> stayed alive an additional four months because
> there were special days he wanted to participate
> in . . . . For two weeks he kept mentioning how
> our big day was going to be soon. We had a
> lovely anniversary, with a big dinner, champagne
> toast, and cake, all served lovingly by my sister.
> He ate, and looked good. After [the celebrations]
> he took to his bed, never to get up again. He
> experienced severe pain five days before his
> death. He wondered why he did not die, except
> that the angels had not appeared to him yet. We
> decided together that the reason the Lord had
> not taken him yet was that the Lord was prepar-

ing us to accept his absence from us and for us to release him to the Lord. That Thursday he rallied, talked all day, had unusual strength for his condition, shared his love with us and his Lord openly. This allowed him the opportunity to share with us through hugs and tears. That night two angels did appear to him at the bottom of his bed. He told us he would not be here tomorrow, and he died at 11:25 A.M. the next day.

This man's lack of pain relates, I'm sure, to the lack of conflict and the peace that everyone involved felt. Tell me—can putting a bag over your head or breathing carbon monoxide do that for a family?

Extraordinary Measures

At a conference recently I was asked, "What do you think of euthanasia?" I somehow do not ever feel that active suicide is appropriate. When the body is tired and doesn't function anymore, then I think it is appropriate to go, to stop nourishing that body and let it die. That is different from putting a gun to your head. I think that suicide can leave an entire family with a message that in the face of adversity, one quits.

When you die naturally you leave something of yourself behind. Committing suicide leaves an emptiness and does not teach others about life and living.

I don't like to see people commit suicide because of what they are afraid of. I'm not against helping people die, in the sense that if they have said, "I'm sore and I'm ready to go," we helped them by not having the family or the nurses yell, "Finish your lunch!" One man said, "I'm in the hospital to die. Why do I have to finish my lunch?" Or we have helped them be sedated so that there was no pain, so they could just relax and let go. In that sense I've helped people. I've helped them release their guilt and not feel like a failure.

I think if choices and power were given back to people, then we would stop worrying about the need to commit suicide because we're afraid we will develop Alzheimer's disease or be in pain.

Don't be afraid of the future—that is really the message. When you get ready, let everybody know. Remember, when the men in Ireland who went on hunger strikes were starving themselves, not eating or drinking, it took them about twenty-three days to die. Well, if you could stop eating and drinking and be dead in twenty-three days, what are you afraid of? What could happen?

What could happen is that people could come in, shove a tube down your throat and start force-feeding you and prevent you from dying. Well, then make out a Living Will, let everybody know what you want, and then you don't have to commit suicide. You can just stop living and let the process complete itself.

This is part of the problem for many people. When we see a book on how to commit suicide become a bestseller, we have to realize that people feel that they have lost their power. They are so worried about living that they are afraid they will not be in control of their dying. What does suicide say to your family? What gift is a death from breathing carbon monoxide?

I am also asked about the other side of the coin: "Under what conditions should doctors take 'extraordinary measures' to sustain life?"

If you think about it, even a heart transplant can be considered an extraordinary measure. We began this century saying, "God save us from diphtheria." We're finishing it saying, "God get me a heart transplant donor." What is an extraordinary measure? I'd say that has a lot to do with the individual. If I still feel that I'm capable of loving and contributing to the world, yes, I'd like people to take extraordinary measures to keep me alive.

I know of a case in which a judge refused to allow a lady in coma to die when her husband and doctor requested it. That lady is well and functioning normally today. I think it is appropriate to use life support measures to keep people alive.

On the other hand, if I'm tired and sore, then an intravenous feeding might be an extraordinary measure, and I can say I don't want it.

So the label "extraordinary" has to do with the stage the individual has reached in his or her life. There are things I as a doctor might not do for somebody who is ninety years old that I might do very easily for somebody who is ten. But I've also tried to resuscitate a ninety-year-old because I knew that he was ready to keep fighting for his life.

The American Association of Retired Persons mentions that the treatment of cancer in the elderly is different from that in younger people, and that perhaps older people are not treated appropriately. I think that has a lot to do with the individual, what "labor pains" he or she is willing to go through at what age. It's not just a matter of blaming the medical profession for not treating people adequately. Perhaps the doctors are thinking of the elderly as people and are being somewhat less aggressive because the treatment might be worse than the disease.

It would be best if each of us made a list of what we call "extraordinary" and allowed our families and physicians to see it—whether that means assisted respiration, transplants, intravenous feeding or a host of other things. We can at least give people an idea of what our philosophy is and of what we would consider important to living, so that one individual who is brought back may ask, "Why did you do this, I want to be dead?" and another who has lost limbs or is paralyzed may still be contributing to the world and will be happy to be alive.

"In essence, we carry within us the love we have received, long after the source of that love has departed from our lives," says John M. Schneider, in an article in the *Noetic Sciences Review*:

> It was Gandhi who stated that grief over the loss of a loved one was perhaps our greatest delusion, for we retain within us the essential character of that relationship. That it is only form, not substance, which is lost is something most of us can only appreciate as a consequence of the experience and grief, not instead of grieving.

In our group meetings, the week after the death of someone who has really lived, has taken on challenges and dealt with afflictions, I have seen a warmth and a wholeness and a fullness in the room even after that person is gone. And when this hasn't happened, there is an emptiness, because we cannot complete the life of someone who is gone.

Michael Lidington, the young man I have mentioned whose cancer recurred, wrote a poem that he asked his brother Ryan to deliver at his funeral service as his final message:

Dare

Twas not there a time,
When a man could be a man?
When a woman could be a woman?
And either one could live without the world?

I see a world with disaster foretold;
I live in a fantasy from times of old
People don't care for silks or gold
No-one's evil, no-one's on parole

I came into this strange world, not knowing up from
down,
It's a world of independence where people need to love.
Do what I have done, and challenge the world
Take nothing for granted, and know where you'regoing

Let go of all your physical restraints, don't rely on any-
thing
This material world won't make it without the love of
God.
Many people care for you or else they wouldn't be here
for you
Trust me, anything is better than no-one

Wipe your tears, I'm having fun.
Do what I did and accept the worst challenge of your
life.
You see, I beat the challenge. I won.
Soon I'll be in a better place of no hate or disease

I'm always with you, so I don't want to see one tear on
your face
You **can** beat the world,
So Challenge it. I DARE YOU.

Michael Charles Lidington died peacefully at home.
He was fifteen years old. After the eulogy, songs, and
poems written for him, he had the last word.

Professor C. Regina Kelley, a sculptor who teaches
at the Maine College of Art, has started a program in
the Hospice Programs in her area. She says:

In traditional cultures, people went to the medicine
person, not only for themselves but to restore harmony to their family and community. When you
look at illness in that light, healing many times
takes place even though the patient dies.

This is something that I have seen over and over

again. A fullness can be left behind. Entire families can be healed by the process of dying of an individual because of what they produced in a spiritual sense as well as sometimes in a physical sense.

If you want to live forever, love someone.

A Joyful Conclusion

Now I would like to share with you two stories that have been significant for me in trying to understand what life is about, what we are here for. One story is about my father, who died recently.

When he died—on June 23, 1991—I learned that we are capable of accomplishing all the things we are talking about. He died at 3:00 P.M. on a Sunday, with a smile on his lips, surrounded by all of the people who loved him who could be there. On Sunday morning, when we arrived at his bedside, I asked my mother to tell me the full story of how they had met, of what had brought these two people together to create this family. And she began to share the humorous account.

While on vacation in Coney Island, New York, with her family, she was sitting on the beach with some girls she didn't know. She said, "Later I learned they had a poor reputation." My father, also on vacation with his family, came down the beach with some teenage boys, and they tossed a coin to see who would get the other girls. And as my mother said, "Your father lost and got me." Well, that began our laughter. I watched my father's color improve with more stories, and a smile appeared on his lips. I had the feeling that at any moment he might open his eyes and say, "I've changed my mind, this is too much fun. I have decided not to die today."

But finally our daughter Carolyn arrived. She was the last person who could make it to his bedside, other grandchildren being in various parts of the country. My father didn't know this consciously because he was semicomatose, but I believe that at a deeper level he was aware of who was coming. Bobbie said, "Carolyn's here." At that moment my father took his last breath and died with a smile on his face.

This was an incredible gift to all of us, particularly to his children and grandchildren, who now have no reason to fear death. One of our children asked me if this was what death was like. I said, "It's what it should be like, but unfortunately generally it is not."

And so I ask you to think about how you too can die with a smile. There is a simple answer. You are surrounded by your family and friends, and you turn to them and say, "Tell stories about our lives." Now, if there is total silence, you're in trouble. And so I am forewarning you to do now some of those wonderful childlike things that everyone will remember and treasure. Of course the key to this, and the key to living between office visits, is to live in the moment—not between anything, not in any limited sense, but right now.

Those memories of my father helped me to let go of my grief. Something else helped, too. A woman at a workshop had given me a book called *Poems That Touch the Heart*, compiled by A. L. Alexander. One day about a week after my father's death I was feeling the pain, the grief, the loss, and I picked up this book and opened it. The story before me was called "The Dark Candle," by Strickland Gillilan.

The story is about a man who is incapable of functioning because his daughter has died. He just can't bring himself to do anything. One day he goes to sleep and dreams that he is in Heaven, where all of the children are marching by with lighted candles. He sees one child way down the line with a dark candle.

So he runs to that child and as he approaches, he realizes it is his daughter. When he gets to her he says, "How is it, darling, that your candle alone is unlighted?" She says, "Father, they often relight it, but your tears always put it out."

That helped me unburden, and go on living.

I learned that rejoicing is the best form of remembrance. Think about what you can do so that you will die with joy in your heart, knowing that you have lived fully and that you have done all that you were meant to do.

What I am asking you to do is to start being and stop playing a part. Don't act, but be. Develop your healing partnerships with physicians, with mates and lovers and friends, so that the marriages, the partnerships, the relationships become healing relationships in which something greater is created, and so that we no longer have to hide ourselves and bury our feelings.

I know that you can continue to heal yourself and to give birth to yourself. Labor can be difficult, but if someone is with you when you are in labor, it becomes much less painful. You respond to that love and that caring and that support.

In your journey understand that God is present. If

you are uncomfortable with the word **God**, substitute **Love**, because when you love, God is a part of your life, invited or not.

And when you get tired, remember to just fall up.

Copyright Acknowledgments

Grateful acknowledgment is made for permission to reprint:

Excerpt from *The Collected Works of C.G. Jung*, translated by R. F. C. Hull, Bollingen Series, Volume 10: *Civilization in Transition*. Copyright © 1960 by Princeton University Press.

Excerpt from *Memories, Dreams, Reflections*, by C. G. Jung, copyright © 1961, 1962, 1963 by Random House, Inc. Published by Pantheon Books, a division of Random House, Inc.

Excerpt from *Health and Medicine in the Jewish Tradition: L'Hayyim—To Life*, by Rabbi David Feldman, copyright © 1986 by Lutheran Institute of Human Ecology. Reprinted by permission of The Crossroad Publishing Company.

226

Excerpts from *Health and Medicine in the Catholic Tradition: Tradition in Transition*, by Richard A. McCormick, copyright © 1984 by Lutheran Institute of Human Ecology. Reprinted by permission of The Crossroad Publishing Company.

Excerpts from "Spirit: Resource for Healing" by Rachel Naomi Remen, from *Noetic Sciences Review*, Autumn 1988, copyright © 1988 by Rachel Naomi Remen. Reprinted by permission of Rachel Naomi Remen, M.D.

Excerpt from "The Transformative Power of Grief" by John M. Schneider, Ph.D., from *Noetic Sciences Review,* Autumn 1989, copyright © 1989 by John M. Schneider, Ph.D. Reprinted by permission of Institute of Noetic Sciences.

Excerpt from "Pop Out of Your Life Drama" by Carol Guion, from *Noetic Sciences Review*, Autumn 1992, copyright © 1992 Institute of Noetic Sciences. Reprinted by permission of Institute of Noetic Sciences.

Lines from "The Death of the Hired Man," by Robert Frost. From *The Poetry of Robert Frost*, edited by Edward Connery Lathen. Published by Henry Holt & Company, Inc., 1969.

Excerpt from "Death of a Salesman," by Arthur Miller, copyright 1949, renewed © 1977 by Arthur Miller. Used by permission of Viking Penguin, a division of Penquin Books, USA Inc.

Excerpts from *My Book for Kids with Cansur*, by Jason Gaes, copyright © 1987 by Jason Gaes. Reprinted by permission of Melius Publishing Corporation—1-800-882-5171.

Excerpt from *Patient Encounters: The Experience of Disease*, by James Buchanan (Charlottesville: Virginia, 1989). Used by permission of the University Press of Virginia.

Excerpt from *The Direction of Human Development* by Ashley Montagu, Chapter 12, pages 288–317, copyright © 1970. Published by Hawthorn Books. Reprinted with the permission of the author.

Excerpt from *Mainstay*, by Maggie Strong, copyright © 1988 by Maggie Strong. Published by Little, Brown and Company.

Excerpts from "First Day," by Robert E. Murphy, published by *The Journal of the American Medical Association*, March 10, 1989, Volume 261, No. 10, page 1509. Copyright © 1989, American Medical Association.

Excerpt from "A Doctor in Her House," by Bernadine Z. Paulshock, M.D., published by *The Journal of the American Medical Association*, January 8, 1992, Volume 267, page 297. Copyright © 1992, American Medical Association.

Excerpts from *Return of the Rishi: A Doctor's Search for the Ultimate Healer*, by Deepak Chopra. Copyright © 1988 by Deepak Chopra, M.D. Reprinted by permission of Houghton Mifflin Co. All rights reserved.

Excerpt from "Write Till You Drop," by Annie Dillard, published in *The New York Times Book Review*, May 28, 1989, copyright © 1989 by Annie Dillard.

Excerpt from *Who Needs God* by Harold Kushner, Copyright © 1989 by Harold S. Kushner. Reprinted by permission of Summit Books, a division of Simon & Schuster, Inc.

Excerpt from *Down from Troy: A Doctor Comes of Age*, by Richard Selzer. Copyright © 1992 by Richard Selzer. Reprinted by permission of William Morrow & Company, Inc.

Excerpts from *Intoxicated By My Illness* by Anatole Broyard. Copyright © 1992 by the Estate of Anatole Broyard. Reprinted by permission of Clarkson N. Potter, Inc., a division of Crown Publishers, Inc.

Excerpt from "Ode to Healing", by John Updike. From *Facing Nature*, by John Updike, copyright © 1985 by John Updike. Reprinted by permission of Alfred A. Knopf, Inc.

Excerpts from *An Open Life: Joseph Campbell in Conversation with Michael Toms*. Copyright © 1988 by New Dimensions Foundations. Reprinted by permission of HarperCollins Publishers Inc.

Excerpts from *The Hero's Journey* by Joseph Campbell edited by Phil Cousineau. Copyright © 1990 by Phil Cousineau. Reprinted by permission of HarperCollins Publishers Inc.

Excerpts from *A Joseph Campbell Companion* edited by Diane Osbon. Copyright © 1992 by Diane Osbon and the Joseph Campbell Foundation. Reprinted by permission of HarperCollins Publishers Inc.

"The Religio-Psychological Dimension of Wounded Healers" by James A. Knight, M.D., B.D., M.P.H., from *Psychiatry and Religion: Overlapping Concerns*, edited by Lillian H. Robinson, M.D. Reprinted by permission of American Psychiatric Press, Inc., Washington, D.C.

Excerpt from *Journey to Ixtlan*, reprinted by permission of the author, Carlos Castenada, and the author's representative, Tracy Kramer, Toltec Artists, Inc., 183 North Martel Avenue, Suite 220, Los Angeles, California 90036. First published in *Journey to Ixtlan*, copyright © 1972.

Excerpts from *The Human Comedy*, copyright 1943 and renewed © 1971 by William Saroyan, reprinted by permission of Harcourt Brace & Company.

ECaP
(Exceptional Cancer Patients)

ECaP (Exceptional Cancer Patients) is the not-for-profit, tax-deductible organization founded by Dr. Siegel in 1978. In the Connecticut area, ECaP offers a clinical program with support group sessions led by psychotherapists. These are available to people who have cancer, AIDS or other chronic or life-challenging illness as a complement to their medical treatments of choice. In addition, each year ECaP sponsors several workshops featuring Dr. Siegel that are open to anyone, with or without health problems.

ECaP offers such services as support group facilitator training workshops and consulting for health professionals.

ECaP publishes a resource directory with valuable information, including Dr. Siegel's national workshop schedule, medical information and more than 150 support service listings and regional referrals where they're available. This guide can be ordered at nominal cost.

All of the books, videotapes and audiocassettes featuring Dr. Siegel can be ordered through ECaP. ECaP also carries many other unique books and health-related guided imagery tapes by other noted experts on healing. To place an order, request a free catalogue of books and tapes or get additional information, please write or call:

ECaP
1302 Chapel Street
New Haven, CT 06511
(203) 865-8392

VIDEOCASSETTES AVAILABLE FEATURING DR. SIEGEL

How to Be Exceptional
ECaP group members and Dr. Siegel share inspirational experiences on healing their lives (1989).
Fight for Your Life
Informative tape with Dr. Siegel and four cancer survivors, who deliver a message of hope and determination.
Hope and a Prayer
Interview with Dr. Siegel that explores his philosophy of healing.
Innervision: Visualizing Super Health
Tape on the many uses of visualization, featuring Dr. Siegel.

GUIDED IMAGERY AUDIOCASSETTES AVAILABLE

Meditations for Overcoming Life's Stresses and Strains
Meditations for Finding the Key to Good Health
Meditations for Enhancing Your Immune System
Meditations for Morning & Evening
Meditations for Healing Your Inner Child
Meditations for Peace of Mind
Getting Ready: Meditations for Surgery, Chemo and Radiation
Meditations for Everyday Living (1988)
Healing Meditations (1988)
Guided Imagery & Meditation (1985)

Affirmation Tapes Available

Healing Partnership Affirmations
Healing Images Affirmations
A Positive New You Affirmations
Finding Your True Self Affirmations

Subliminal Tapes Available

Healing Through Surgery
Health & Well Being
Chemotherapy and Healing
Radiation and Healing
Caring and Caregivers
Note: On the subliminal tapes, you'll hear only music, Pachelbel's "Canon."

About the Author

Dr. BERNARD S. SIEGEL, who prefers to be called Bernie, not Dr. Siegel, attended Colgate University and Cornell University Medical College. He holds membership in two scholastic honor societies, Phi Beta Kappa and Alpha Omega Alpha, and graduated with honors. His surgical training took place at Yale New Haven Hospital and the Children's Hospital of Pittsburgh. He practiced general and pediatric surgery in New Haven, Connecticut, until 1989, when he retired.

In 1978, Bernie started Exceptional Cancer Patients (ECaP), a specific form of individual and group therapy using patients' dreams, drawings and images. ECaP is based on "carefrontation," a loving, safe, therapeutic confrontation that facilitates personal change and healing. This experience led to his desire to make everyone aware of his or her own healing potential.

The Siegel family lives in the New Haven area. Bernie and his wife, Bobbie Siegel, have co-written many articles and have five children. The family has innumerable interests and pets. Their home resembles a cross between a family art gallery, a zoo, a museum and an automobile repair shop.

In 1986, his first book, *Love, Medicine & Miracles*, and in 1989 his second book, *Peace, Love & Healing*, were published. These events redirected his life. He is now very involved in humanizing medical care and medical education and teaching the health-care professions about the mind–body connection. Bernie travels extensively with Bobbie to speak and run workshops sharing his techniques and experience.

His prediction is that in a decade the effects of consciousness on humans and matter will be an accepted scientific fact and that patients will be active participants in the health care of the future.

HarperAudio
A Division of HarperCollins*Publishers*

<u>*Bernie Siegel on Cassette*</u>

"Hearing what the good doctor has to say is most effective;
it's as if you and he are having a personal seminar."

— *Publishers Weekly* on *Love, Medicine & Miracles*

*Listen to the wisdom and warmth of
Bernie Siegel on audio cassette.*

How to Live Between Office Visits
ISBN: 1-55994-740-3
2 cassettes / 3 Hours
$17.00

Love, Medicine & Miracles
ISBN: 0-89845-767-X
2 cassettes / 3 Hours
$16.95

Peace, Love & Healing
ISBN: 0-89845-918-4
2 cassettes / 3 Hours
$16.00

Personal Reflections and Meditations
ISBN: 1-55994-430-7
1 cassette / 1 Hour
$10.00

At your bookstore or call 1(800) 331-3761.